The Great Machines

POEMS AND SONGS

OF THE AMERICAN RAILROAD

EDITED BY ROBERT HEDIN

University of Iowa Press Ψ Iowa City

University of Iowa Press, Iowa City 52242

Library of Congress Cataloging-in-Publication Data
The great machines: poems and songs of the American railroad / edited by
Robert Hedin.
p.   cm.
Includes index.
ISBN 0-87745-550-3 (paper)
1. Railroad travel—United States—Poetry.   2. Railroads—United
States—Poetry.   3. Songs, English—United States—Texts.
4. American poetry.   I. Hedin, Robert, 1949–
PS595.R325G73   1996
811.008′0355—dc20   95-50142
                                                                 CIP

01 · 00   99   98   97   96   P   5   4   3   2   1

For my mother, Elizabeth

They move dark as our destiny, immense as love.

—John Frederick Nims

CONTENTS

VI. Coach Trains across the Seamless Land

VII. The Twilight Gray as Steel

To countless Americans of not so long ago, the railroad was much more than the historic curiosity it is today. To many, it represented the very spirit of America itself, and its bold, uncompromising presence meant change, modernity, and an unchecked future.

More than any other innovation of the nineteenth century, the railroad helped shape the American experience, transforming the wilderness into civilization, the country into a nation of consolidated lands, and it redefined in almost inexplicable ways our fundamental notions of time, distance, and community, if not the very nature of ourselves. Indeed, the histories of the railroad and of America are so inextricably bound they are essentially one and the same. For generations the railroad was, as Walt Whitman characterized it, "the pulse of the continent," reigning supreme as the dynamic symbol of an expanding American empire.

The long and storied history of the railroad in the United States dates from 1829 when the first locomotives were imported from England by Horatio Allen for the Delaware & Hudson Canal Company. Being little more than boilers on wheels, they were nothing compared to the enormous steam engines that would roam the American landscape a hundred years later, some so long they would have to be hinged at the girth in order to pass around mountain curves. For many, in fact, these crude seven-ton contraptions proved to be sources of ridicule, and few at the time believed they could ever wrestle the control of the booming trade routes of the Northeast from the canalboat and the newly opened Erie Canal.

Following the first successful run of the *Tom Thumb*, a much sleeker locomotive built by inventor Peter Cooper in 1830, many short-run railroads began to appear, and by 1835 more than 200 rail lines were in design or construction, with over 1,000 miles of track in operation. By 1850, railroad investments in the country had reached nearly $4,000,000, and the total mileage nationwide had grown to almost 9,000, easily surpassing that of the canals. The eastern seaboard was linked to the Great Lakes in 1850, to Chicago in 1853, and to the western side of the Mississippi in 1856.

By the time the Civil War broke out, over 31,000 miles of track were in operation, two-thirds of which lay in the hands of the North, a factor that ultimately helped decide the outcome of the war. It was the first war in history in which the railroad played a major role, able to transport large numbers of troops and supplies hundreds of miles in order to do battle.

The building of the first transcontinental railroad, an epic venture begun in 1867 and completed in 1869 with the driving of the golden spike at Promontory, Utah, ranks as perhaps the single greatest industrial feat in all of American history. With the Union Pacific Railroad working westward from Omaha and the Central Pacific building eastward from Sacramento, thousands of Chinese and Irish immigrants bridged, graded, blasted, and tunneled their way across 1,800 miles of forbidding terrain, sending out over the vast American frontier a strange industrial music never before heard, a "Grand Anvil Chorus," as one journalist called it, done "in triple time, three strokes to a spike."

In the decades following the completion of the first overland route, the total mileage of track in the country continued to climb, due largely to the opening of the West for settlement and exploitation and to the rapid growth of industrialism. By 1880, for instance, there were 94,000 miles of rails nationwide; by 1900, 193,000. Such figures increased steadily until 1930 when America could boast to the world of its nearly 430,000 miles of track and its more than 1,000 operating railroads.

It was not until the growth of the aviation, automobile, and trucking industries following World War II, however, that the railroad in America began its decline. Track mileage shrank, long-distance passenger service decreased, and many small, regional lines disappeared altogether. Though it still controls a healthy share of the freight business in America today, there is little doubt that the rail industry as a whole has lost much of its vision and energy, having fallen prey to a world that is fiercely efficient in its drive for greater and faster mobility and communication.

Years from now, after the last of the crack express trains has been shuttled off to the scrap heaps, perhaps someone will look back in awe and curiosity and wonder how this genial and once-flourishing way of travel could have fallen to such a beleaguered state. Indeed, the railroad was one of the cornerstones of our culture, and for generations its presence had a galvanizing effect upon the entire country, helping define and sustain our culture physically and spiritually. Without it, our nation would have lacked the essential tool it needed to successfully make the leap from uncharted wilderness to global power.

The Great Machines presents the scope and variety of poems and songs written about the American railroad in the last one hundred and fifty years. Composed of selections from both the written and the oral traditions of American literature, the volume celebrates the literary, historical, and cultural significance of this marvel of engineering skills, evoking its haunting presence in particular, palpable ways. Gathered are work songs, ballads, spirituals, hymns, blues, and hobo songs as well as a significant number of poems by many of our nation's premier poets. Together, they chart the railroad's course from an industrial innovation to a cultural phenomenon to its present status as a symbol of a vanishing way of life in America. Ultimately, the volume provides a compelling portrait of the railroad, offering a wide range of themes, attitudes, and perspectives of what historian J. H. Clapham has called "the industrial revolution incarnate."

While several of the poets in the volume reveal a fascination with the sheer physical magnitude of the train, seeing in its brute tonnage and thundering noise a kind of divinely inspired creation, others employ the railroad as a means to explore particular facets of America's cultural history. Walt Whitman, for example, views the "black cylindric body, golden brass and silvery steel" of the nineteenth-century locomotive as an "emblem of motion and power" that would launch America on its quest for manifest destiny. Vachel Lindsay and John Neihardt, on the other hand, portray the train's impact upon the West and on our Native American cultures, depicting the massive changes that occurred across the frontier once the first transcontinental railroad was completed. Others such as Robert Hayden, Dudley Randall, and Langston Hughes deal with the train's place in African American history, offering several terse reminders of the deep racial divisions in America prior to the arrival of the civil rights movement in the 1960s, what Hughes symbolically calls "the freedom train."

Some of the richest pieces in the volume are the many ballads and work songs that rose out of the massive construction of our nation's railroads during the nineteenth century. Handed down from one generation to another, they occupy a unique place in our culture's folkloric traditions and still remain enormously popular today. "Poor Paddy Works on the Railway" and "Drill, Ye Tarriers, Drill," for example, commemorate the hardiness of the thousands of Irish section crews who labored as track layers, gaugers, spikers, and bolters, while others such as "Tamping Ties," "Railroad Section Leader's Song," and "Take This Hammer" were chanted by black work gangs during the reconstruction of the South following the Civil War. Filled with pride and rebelliousness and driven by the muscular rhythms of the body at work, they constitute some of the finest examples of work songs that we have in this country. At the same time, the collection brings together such legendary figures as John Henry, Casey Jones, and Railroad Bill—all heroes of balladic cycles and tall tales of the same era.

Because the train and the blues have always been closely aligned, both playing significant roles in the composition of black life in the Deep South, *The Great Machines* also presents a number of blues lyrics and poems from both the oral and the written traditions. Unique, powerful, and full of emotional range, each is a distinctly individual expression in which the train holds a commanding presence, its driving rhythms and counter-rhythms complementing the themes of sorrow, suffering, or lost love. To read Sterling Brown's "Long Track Blues" or Bill Monroe's version of "In the Pines," for example, is to be reminded again of how utterly fascinating and enduring the blues are, a medium that has been able to make the leap from oral to written traditions without sacrificing any of its appeal or artistic integrity.

At the same time, the volume offers several hobo songs—"The Wabash Cannonball," "Hallelujah, Bum Again," and "The Big Rock Candy Mountains"—all of which have achieved lasting reputations and speak with authenticity of the oftentimes perilous lives of the migrant workers who rode boxcars during the Dust Bowl days of the Great Depression. Though all three are considered classics in their own right, "The Big Rock Candy Mountains" is perhaps the most renowned. With its beatific vision of a land of cigarette trees, lemonade springs, fountains of soda water, and nothing but balmy weather, it has survived for decades as a kind of hobo anthem. On the other hand, "Hallelujah, Bum Again" is governed by a defiant tone and was picked up by the Industrial Workers of the World to help build morale among unskilled workers during the rise of unionized labor in America in the early 1900s.

The Great Machines also contains several poems and songs dealing with our continual fascination with train disasters. "Wreck of the Old 97," for instance, has enjoyed enormous popularity for years and rises from traditions developed around Appalachia from the Civil War to World War I. Others such as T. R. Hummer's "Train Wreck, 1890," John Frederick Nims's "Trainwrecked Soldiers," and Hayden Carruth's "The Wreck of the Circus Train" successfully carry such traditions into the world of contemporary poetry and reveal an equal fascination with all the terror-struck bucklings and steel wrenchings of ill-fated trains.

A surprising number of selections in the volume equate the railroad with death, a perception that rose from the notion of terminals and funeral trains as well as from the obvious symbolic links between a train's arrival and departure and a person's own birth and death. Such southern hymns as "The Beulah Railway," "The Gospel Train," and "Little Black Train Is A-Comin'" tend to depict the railroad in allegorical terms, as a foreboding but ultimately glorious vehicle waiting to carry the dead to an afterlife where nothing but freedom and equality abound. Others such as "The Black Train" by Thomas McGrath, "Lucifer in the Train" by Adrienne Rich, and "A Sister on the Tracks" by Donald Hall render the railroad in more metaphysical ways, as a bridge to temporal and eternal worlds, a "vertical track," as Hall writes, "that rises from the underworld of graves" to connect the living and the dead.

A great many of the poems in The Great Machines devote themselves to the exhilaration and enthusiasm of train travel itself, the poets assuming that quintessentially American pose of being footloose and free. Some such as the selection from "The Bridge" by Hart Crane, "Campaign" by Muriel Rukeyser, and "Starting from San Francisco" by Lawrence Ferlinghetti deal with long transcontinental journeys in search of the American spirit. Others deal with more personal and intimate journeys. "In Cheever Country" by Dana Gioia and "The Old Trip by Dream Train" by Brendan Galvin, for example, deal with train trips home, back to what Gioia calls "the modest places which contain our lives." All in one way or another remind us that train travel makes us aware of a larger world, one of various landscapes and ways of life that are oftentimes very different from our own. Unlike air travel with its coldly detached view of the world, trains, they remind us, keep us close to the ground, linked to the land's every rhythm and subtlety. On trains, nearly every conceivable form of topography is experienced, the land passing cinematically by in a rush of impressions, a continuous narrative that has for many an almost epical feel. One arrives filled with all sorts of terrains and a keener sense of the sheer breadth and magnitude of the American landscape.

Moreover, as many in *The Great Machines* suggest, the train provides glimpses into the many facets of American domestic and working life, from backyards to industrial sites, from small towns to sprawling metropolitan centers. Its passengers, in other words, are allowed to see how America lives, to look voyeuristically "through wreaths of engine smoke," as Robert Frost writes, "far into the lives of other folk." Furthermore, it is communal and carries from place to place a broad spectrum of the American community. Riding on trains, travelers have to be open to their neighbors, open to that traditional sense of sharing.

The Great Machines concludes with a number of selections dealing with the decline of the railroad era in America. In such poems as "Riding the Rock Island through Kansas" by Dave Etter, "The Tie" by William Heyen, "The Last Train" by Linda Pastan, and "Grazing Locomotives" by Archibald MacLeish, tracks are being sold off, crossties are being torn up, and depots are being turned into what James Wright calls "great clanging cathedrals of rust and smoke." Everywhere, in other words, the dismantling of an era is evident. If historians have traced the social, economic, and political reasons for the decline of this oldest and most honored means of inland travel in America, it is our nation's poets who have provided a poignant benediction, seeing in the dying of our trains the loss of a uniquely American way of life, if not a worldview.

Ultimately, *The Great Machines* offers some 140 pieces of a highly intricate puzzle that when put together form an accurate and compelling portrait of the American railroad and the era in which it reigned supreme. Many of the poems and songs throughout the volume are readily identifiable and still enjoy considerable popularity today. Others are not as well known and many readers will be introduced to them for the first time. No attempt has been made to create any artificial divisions between oral and written poetries. Instead, they have been placed side by side in the hope that they will overlap in theme and sensibility, one tradition shedding a revealing light upon the other. Together, they evoke the unique spirit of the railroad as well as a time in our nation's history when the whole continent, every shape and contour, was alive with the ghost-smoke of trains.

I. LAYING THE

LONG RAILS DOWN

Hear ye, Dakotas! When the Great Father at Washington sent us his chief soldier to ask for a path through our hunting grounds, a way for his iron road to the mountains and the western sea, we were told that they wished merely to pass through our country, not to tarry among us, but to seek gold in the far west.
—Chief Red Cloud

I see over my own continent the Pacific railroad surmounting every barrier,
I see continual trains of cars winding along the Platte carrying freight and
*   passengers,*
I hear the locomotives rushing and roaring, and the shrill steam whistle,
I hear the echoes reverberate through the grandest scenery in the world . . .
—Walt Whitman, from "Passage to India"

CHRISTOPHER PEARSE CRANCH

from SEVEN WONDERS OF THE WORLD

THE LOCOMOTIVE

Whirling along its living freight, it came,
Hot, panting, fierce, yet docile to command—
The roaring monster, blazing through the land
Athwart the night, with crest of smoke and flame;
Like those weird bulls Medea learned to tame
By sorcery, yoked to plough the Colchian strand
In forced obedience under Jason's hand.
Yet modern skill outstripped this antique fame,
When o'er our plains and through the rocky bar
Of hills it pushed its ever-lengthening line
Of iron roads, with gain far more divine
Than when the daring Argonauts from far
Came for the golden fleece, which like a star
Hung clouded in the dragon-guarded shrine.

WALT WHITMAN

TO A LOCOMOTIVE IN WINTER

Thee for my recitative,
Thee in the driving storm even as now, the snow, the winter-day
    declining,
Thee in thy panoply, thy measur'd dual throbbing and thy beat
    convulsive,
Thy black cylindric body, golden brass and silvery steel,
Thy ponderous side-bars, parallel and connecting rods, gyrating,
    shuttling at thy sides,
Thy metrical, now swelling pant and roar, now tapering in the
    distance,
Thy great protruding head-light fix'd in front,
Thy long, pale, floating vapor-pennants, tinged with delicate purple,
The dense and murky clouds out-belching from thy smoke-stack,
Thy knitted frame, thy springs and valves, the tremulous twinkle of
    thy wheels,
Thy train of cars behind, obedient, merrily following,
Through gale or calm, now swift, now slack, yet steadily careering;
Type of the modern—emblem of motion and power—pulse of the
    continent,
For once come serve the Muse and merge in verse, even as here I
    see thee,
With storm and buffeting gusts of wind and falling snow,
By day thy warning ringing bell to sound its notes,
By night thy silent signal lamps to swing.

Fierce-throated beauty!
Roll through my chant with all thy lawless music, thy swinging lamps
    at night,
Thy madly-whistled laughter, echoing, rumbling like an earthquake,
    rousing all,

⟨ 4 ⟩

Law of thyself complete, thine own track firmly holding,
(No sweetness debonair of tearful harp or glib piano thine,)
Thy trills of shrieks by rocks and hills return'd,
Launch'd o'er the prairies wide, across the lakes,
To the free skies unpent and glad and strong.

EMILY DICKINSON
_____

I LIKE TO SEE IT LAP THE MILES
_____

I like to see it lap the Miles—
And lick the Valleys up—
And stop to feed itself at Tanks—
And then—prodigious step

Around a Pile of Mountains—
And supercilious peer
In Shanties—by the sides of Roads—
And then a Quarry pare

To fit its Ribs
And crawl between
Complaining all the while
In horrid—hooting stanza—
Then chase itself down Hill—

And neigh like Boanerges—
Then—punctual as a Star
Stop—docile and omnipotent
At its own stable door—

HENRY DAVID THOREAU

WHAT'S THE RAILROAD TO ME?

What's the railroad to me?
I never go to see
Where it ends.
It fills a few hollows,
And makes banks for the swallows,
It sets the sand a-blowing,
And the blackberries a-growing . . .

ANONYMOUS

TAMPING TIES

Tamp 'em up solid,
All the livelong day.
Tamp 'em up solid,
Then they'll hold that midnight mail.
The captain don't like me.
Won't allow me no show.
Well, work don't hurt me,
Don't care where in the world I go.

⟨6⟩

Work don't hurt me,
Like the early rise.
Well, work don't hurt me,
But that's the thing that hurts my pride,
That hurts my pride,
That hurts my pride,
That hurts my pride.

ANONYMOUS

RAILROAD SECTION LEADER'S SONG

Ef ah could, ah sholy would,
Stan on da rock whuh Moses stood.

Mary, Martha, Luke an John,
All dem sciples dead an gon.

Ah gotta woman in Jennielee Square,
Ef you wanna die easy, lemme ketch you there.

Lil Evaline, settin in da shade,
Figurin on da money I ain't made.

Jack de rabbit, Jack de bear,
Cancha move it jus a hair?

All ah hate bout linin track,
Dese ol bars bout to break mah back.

You keep talkin bout da joint ahead,
Never say nawthin bout mah hog an bread.

Way down yonder in da holla of da fiel,
Angels wukkin on da chayet wheel.

Reason I stay wid my cap'n so long,
He giv me biscuits to rear back on.

Jes lemme tell ya whut da cap'n jes done,
Looked at his watch and he looked at da sun.

    Ho, Boys, it ain't time.
    Ho, Boys, you cain't quit.
    Ho, Boys, it ain time.
    Sun ain gone down yit.

LEADBELLY

TAKE THIS HAMMER

Take this hammer, (huh!) carry it to the captain, (huh!)
Take this hammer, (huh!) carry it to the captain, (huh!)
Take this hammer, (huh!) carry it to the captain, (huh!)
Tell him I'm gone, (huh!) tell him I'm gone. (huh!)

If he asks you, (huh!) was I running, (huh!)
If he asks you, (huh!) was I running, (huh!)
If he asks you, (huh!) was I running, (huh!)
Tell him I was flying, (huh!) tell him I was flying. (huh!)

If he asks you, (huh!) was I laughing, (huh!)
If he asks you, (huh!) was I laughing, (huh!)
If he asks you, (huh!) was I laughing, (huh!)
Tell him I was crying, (huh!) tell him I was crying. (huh!)

Take this hammer, (huh!) and carry it to the captain, (huh!)
Take this hammer, (huh!) and carry it to the captain, (huh!)
Take this hammer, (huh!) and carry it to the captain, (huh!)
Tell him I'm gone, (huh!) tell him I'm gone. (huh!)

STERLING A. BROWN

SOUTHERN ROAD

Swing dat hammer—hunh—
Steady, bo';
Swing dat hammer—hunh—
Steady, bo';
Ain't no rush, bebby,
Long ways to go.

Burner tore his—hunh—
Black heart away;
Burner tore his—hunh—
Black heart away;
Got me life, bebby,
An' a day.

Gal's on Fifth Street—hunh—
Son done gone;

Gal's on Fifth Street—hunh—
Son done gone;
Wife's in de ward, bebby,
Babe's not bo'n.

My ole man died—hunh—
Cussin' me;
My ole man died—hunh—
Cussin' me;
Ole lady rocks, bebby,
Huh misery.

Doubleshackled—hunh—
Guard behin';
Doubleshackled—hunh—
Guard behin';
Ball an' chain, bebby,
On my min'.

White man tells me—hunh—
Damn yo' soul,
White man tells me—hunh—
Damn yo' soul;
Got no need, bebby,
To be tole.

Chain gang nevah—hunh—
Let me go;
Chain gang nevah—hunh—
Let me go;
Po' los' boy, bebby,
Evahmo'. . . .

ANONYMOUS
_____

JOHN HENRY
_____

John Henry was a li'l baby, un-huh,
Sittin' on his mama's knee, oh, yeah.
Said: "De Big Bend Tunnel on de C. & O. road
Gonna cause de death of me,
Lawd, Lawd, gonna' cause de death of me."

John Henry, he had a woman,
Her name was Mary Magdalene,
She would go to de tunnel and sing for John,
Jes' to hear John Henry's hammer ring,
Lawd, Lawd, jes' to hear John Henry's hammer ring.

John Henry had a li'l woman,
Her name was Lucy Ann,
John Henry took sick an' had to go to bed,
Lucy Ann drove steel like a man,
Lawd, Lawd, Lucy Ann drove steel like a man.

Cap'n says to John Henry,
"Gonna bring me a steam drill 'round,
Gonna take dat steam drill out on de job,
Gonna whop dat steel on down,
Lawd, Lawd, gonna whop dat steel on down."

John Henry tol' his cap'n,
Lightnin' was in his eye:
"Cap'n, bet yo' las' red cent on me,
Fo' I'll beat it to de bottom or I'll die,
Lawd, Lawd, I'll beat it to de bottom or I'll die."

Sun shine hot an' burnin',
Wer'n't no breeze a-tall,
Sweat ran down like water down a hill,
Dat day John Henry let his hammer fall,
Lawd, Lawd, dat day John Henry let his hammer fall.

John Henry went to de tunnel,
An' dey put him in de lead to drive;
De rock so tall an' John Henry so small,
Dat he lied down his hammer an' he cried,
Lawd, Lawd, dat he lied down his hammer an' he cried.

John Henry started on de right hand,
De steam drill started on de lef'—
"Before I'd let dis steam drill beat me down,
I'd hammer my fool self to death,
Lawd, Lawd, I'd hammer my fool self to death."

White man tol' John Henry,
"Nigger, damn yo' soul,
You might beat dis steam an' drill of mine,
When de rocks in dis mountain turn to gol',
Lawd, Lawd, when de rocks in dis mountain turn to gol'."

John Henry said to his shaker,
"Nigger, why don' you sing?
I'm throwin' twelve poun's from my hips on down,
Jes' listen to de col' steel ring,
Lawd, Lawd, jes' listen to de col' steel ring."

Oh, de captain said to John Henry,
"I b'lieve this mountain's shakin' in."
John Henry said to his captain, oh my,
"Ain' nothin' but my hammer suckin' win'.
Lawd, Lawd, ain' nothin' but my hammer suckin' win'."

John Henry tol' his shaker,
"Shaker, you better pray,
For, if I miss dis six-foot steel,

Tomorrow'll be yo' buryin' day,
Lawd, Lawd, tomorrow'll be yo' buryin' day."

John Henry tol' his captain,
"Looka yonder what I see—
Yo' drill's done broke an' yo' hole's done choke,
An' you cain' drive steel like me,
Lawd, Lawd, an' you cain' drive steel like me."

De man dat invented de steam drill,
Thought he was mighty fine.
John Henry drove his fifteen feet,
An' de steam drill only made nine,
Lawd, Lawd, an' de steam drill only made nine.

De hammer dat John Henry swung
It weighed over nine pound;
He broke a rib in his lef'-han' side,
An' his intrels fell on de groun',
Lawd, Lawd, an' his intrels fell on de groun'.

John Henry was hammerin' on de mountain,
An' his hammer was strikin' fire,
He drove so hard till he broke his pore heart,
An' he lied down his hammer an' he died,
Lawd, Lawd, he lied down his hammer and he died.

All de womens in de Wes',
When de heared of John Henry's death,
Stood in de rain, flagged de eas'-boun' train,
Goin' where John Henry fell dead,
Lawd, Lawd, goin' where John Henry fell dead.

John Henry's li'l mother,
She was all dressed in red,
She jumped in bed, covered up her head,
Said she didn' know her son was dead,
Lawd, Lawd, didn' know her son was dead.

John Henry had a pretty li'l woman,
An' de dress she wo' was blue,
An' de las' words she said to him:
"John Henry, I've been true to you,
Lawd, Lawd, John Henry, I've been true to you."

ANONYMOUS
——————————

POOR PADDY WORKS ON THE RAILWAY
———————————————————————

Oh in eighteen hundred and forty-one
My corduroy britches I put on,
My corduroy britches I put on,
To work upon the railway, the railway,
I'm weary of the railway;
Oh poor Paddy works on the railway!

Oh in eighteen hundred and forty-two
I did not know what I should do,
I did not know what I should do,
To work upon the railway, the railway,
I'm weary of the railway;
Oh poor Paddy works on the railway!

Oh in eighteen hundred and forty-three
I sailed away across the sea,
I sailed away across the sea,
To work upon the railway, the railway,
I'm weary of the railway;
Oh poor Paddy works on the railway!

⟨ 14 ⟩

Oh in eighteen hundred and forty-four
I landed on Columbia's shore,
I landed on Columbia's shore,
To work upon the railway, the railway,
I'm weary of the railway;
Oh poor Paddy works on the railway!

Oh in eighteen hundred and forty-five
When Daniel O'Connell he was alive,
When Daniel O'Connell he was alive,
To work upon the railway, the railway,
I'm weary of the railway;
Oh poor Paddy works on the railway!

Oh in eighteen hundred and forty-six
I changed my trade to carrying bricks,
I changed my trade to carrying bricks,
From working on the railway, the railway,
I was weary of the railway;
Oh poor Paddy worked on the railway!

Oh in eighteen hundred and forty-seven
Poor Paddy was thinking of going to Heaven,
Poor Paddy was thinking of going to Heaven,
After working on the railway, the railway,
He was weary of the railway;
Oh poor Paddy worked on the railway!

THOMAS CASEY

DRILL, YE TARRIERS, DRILL

Ev'ry morning at seven o'clock
There's twenty tarriers a-working at the rock.
And the boss comes along and he says, "kape still,
And come down heavy with the cast iron drill."
And drill, ye tarriers, drill!

> *Chorus:*
> Drill, ye tarriers, drill. It's work all day
>   for the sugar in your tay,
> Down behind the railway. And drill, ye tarriers,
>   drill, and blast, and fire.

Now our new foreman was Jean McCann,
By God, he was a blame mean man.
Past week, a premature blast went off
And a mile in the air went big Jim Goff,
And drill, ye tarriers, drill!

Now the next time payday comes around,
Jim Goff a dollar short was found.
When asked, "What for?" came this reply,
"You're docked for the time you was up in the sky."
And drill, ye tarriers, drill!

Now the boss was a fine man, down to the ground,
And he married a lady, six feet round.
She baked good bread and she baked it well,
But she baked it hard as the holes of hell.
And drill, ye tarriers, drill!

MALCOLM COWLEY

BLUE JUNIATA

Farmhouses curl like horns of plenty, hide
scrawny bare shanks against a barn, or crouch
empty in the shadow of a mountain. Here
there is no house at all—

only the bones of a house,
lilacs growing beside them,
roses in clumps between them,
honeysuckle over;
a gap for a door, a chimney
mud-chinked, an immense fireplace,
the skeleton of a pine,

and gandy dancers working on the rails
that run not thirty yards from the once door.

I heard a gandy dancer playing on a jew's harp
Where is now that merry party I remember long ago?
Nelly was a lady . . . twice . . . *Old Black Joe,*
as if he laid his right hand on my shoulder,
saying, "Your father lived here long ago,
your father's father built the house, lies buried
under the pine—"
                    Sing *Nelly was a lady*
. . . *Blue Juniata* . . . *Old Black Joe:*

for sometimes a familar music hammers
like blood against the eardrums, paints a mist
across the eyes, as if the smell of lilacs,
moss roses, and the past became a music
made visible, a monument of air.

CARL SANDBURG

WORK GANGS

Box cars run by a mile long.
And I wonder what they say to each other
When they stop a mile long on a sidetrack.
    Maybe their chatter goes:
I came from Fargo with a load of wheat up to the danger line.
I came from Omaha with a load of shorthorns and they splintered
    my boards.
I came from Detroit heavy with a load of flivvers.
I carried apples from the Hood River last year and this year bunches
    of bananas from Florida; they look for me with watermelons from
    Mississippi next year.

Hammers and shovels of work gangs sleep in shop corners
when the dark stars come on the sky and the night watchmen walk
    and look.

Then the hammer heads talk to the handles,
then the scoops of the shovels talk,
how the day's work nicked and trimmed them,
how they swung and lifted all day,
how the hands of the work gangs smelled of hope.
In the night of the dark stars
when the curve of the sky is a work gang handle,
in the night on the mile long sidetracks,
in the night where the hammers and shovels sleep in corners,
the night watchmen stuff their pipes with dreams—
and sometimes they doze and don't care for nothin',
and sometimes they search their heads for meanings, stories, stars.
    The stuff of it runs like this:

A long way we come; a long way to go; long rests and long deep sniffs
    for our lungs on the way.
Sleep is a belonging of all; even if all songs are old songs and the
    singing heart is snuffed out like a switchman's lantern with the oil
    gone, even if we forget our names and houses in the finish, the
    secret of sleep is left us, sleep belongs to all, sleep is the first and
    last and best of all.

People singing; people with song mouths connecting with song hearts;
    people who must sing or die; people whose song hearts break if
    there is no song mouth; these are my people.

ARCHIBALD MACLEISH

BURYING GROUND BY THE TIES

Ayee! Ai! This is heavy earth on our shoulders:
There were none of us born to be buried in this earth:
Niggers we were, Portuguese, Magyars, Polacks:

We were born to another look of the sky certainly.
Now we lie here in the river pastures:
We lie in the mowings under the thick turf:

We hear the earth and the all-day rasp of the grasshoppers.
It was we laid the steel to this land from ocean to ocean:
It was we (if you know) put the U. P. through the passes

Bringing her down into Laramie full load,
Eighteen mile on the granite anticlinal,
Forty-three foot to the mile and the grade holding:

It was we did it: hunkies of our kind.
It was we dug the caved-in holes for the cold water:
It was we built the gully spurs and the freight sidings:

Who would do it but we and the Irishmen bossing us?
It was all foreign-born men there were in this country:
It was Scotsmen, Englishmen, Chinese, Squareheads, Austrians . . .

Ayee! but there's weight to the earth under it.
Not for this did we come out—to be lying here
Nameless under the ties in the clay cuts:

There's nothing good in the world but the rich will buy it:
Everything sticks to the grease of a gold note—
Even a continent—even a new sky!

Do not pity us much for the strange grass over us:
We laid the steel to the stone stock of these mountains:
The place of our graves is marked by the telegraph poles!

It was not to lie in the bottoms we came out
And the trains going over us here in the dry hollows . . .

CARL SANDBURG

SOUTHERN PACIFIC

Huntington sleeps in a house six feet long.
Huntington dreams of railroads he built and owned.
Huntington dreams of ten thousand men saying: Yes, sir.

Blithery sleeps in a house six feet long.
Blithery dreams of rails and ties he laid.
Blithery dreams of saying to Huntington: Yes, sir.

Huntington,
Blithery, sleep in houses six feet long.

ARCHIBALD MACLEISH

from EMPIRE BUILDERS

THE MUSEUM ATTENDANT

This is *The Making of America in Five Panels*:

This is Mister Harriman making America:
Mister-Harriman-is-buying-the-Union-Pacific-at-Seventy:
The Sante Fe is shining on his hair.

This is Commodore Vanderbilt making America:
Mister-Vanderbilt-is-eliminating-the-short-interest-in-Hudson:
Observe the carving on the rocking chair.

This is J. P. Morgan making America:
(The Tennessee Coal is behind to the left of the Steel Company.)
Those in mauve are braces he is wearing.

This is Mister Mellon making America:
Mister-Mellon-is-represented-as-a-symbolical-figure-in-aluminum-
Strewing-bank-stocks-on-a-burnished-stair.

This is the Bruce is the Barton making America:
Mister-Barton-is-selling-us-Doctor's-Deliciousest-Dentifrice.
This is he in beige with the canary.

You have just beheld the Makers making America:
This is The Making of America in Five Panels:
America lies to the west-southwest of the switch-tower:
There is nothing to see of America but land.

JOHN NEIHARDT

from THE SONG OF THE INDIAN WARS

Summer turned.
Where blackbirds chattered and the scrub oaks burned
In meadows of the Milk and Musselshell,
The fatted bison sniffed the winter-smell

Beneath the whetted stars, and drifted south.
Across the Yellowstone, lean-ribbed with drouth,
The living rivers bellowed, morn to morn.
The Powder and the Rosebud and the Horn
Flowed backward freshets, roaring to their heads.
Now up across the Cheyenne watersheds
The manless cattle wrangled day and night.
Along the Niobrara and the White
Uncounted thirsts were slaked. The peace that broods
Aloof among the sandhill solitudes
Fled from the bawling bulls and lowing cows.
Along the triple Loup they paused to browse
And left the lush sloughs bare. Along the Platte
The troubled myriads pawed the sandy flat
And snorted at the evil men had done.
For there, from morning sun to evening sun,
A strange trail cleft the ancient bison world,
And many-footed monsters whirred and whirled
Upon it; many-eyed they blinked, and screamed;
Tempestuous with speed, the long mane streamed
Behind them; and the breath of them was loud—
A rainless cloud with lightning in the cloud
And alien thunder.
                    Thus the driving breed,
The bold earth-takers, toiled to make the deed
Audacious as the dream. One season saw
The steel trail crawl away from Omaha
As far as ox-rigs waddled in a day—
An inchworm bound for San Francisco Bay!
The next beheld a brawling, sweating host
Of men and mules build on to Kearney Post
While spring greens mellowed into winter browns,
And prairie dogs were giving up their towns
To roaring cities. Where the Platte divides,
The metal serpent sped, with league-long strides,
Between two winters. North Platte City sprang
From sage brush where the prairie sirens sang
Of magic bargains in the marts of lust;
A younger Julesburg sprouted from the dust

To howl a season at the panting trains;
Cheyenne, begotten of the ravished plains,
All-hailed the planet as the steel clanged by.
And now in frosty vacancies of sky
The rail-head waited spring on Sherman Hill,
And, brooding further prodigies of will,
Blinked off at China.

VACHEL LINDSAY

———————————————

THE FLOWER-FED BUFFALOES

———————————————

The flower-fed buffaloes of the spring
In the days of long ago,
Ranged where the locomotives sing
And the prairie flowers lie low:—
The tossing, blooming, perfumed grass
Is swept away by the wheat,
Wheels and wheels and wheels spin by
In the spring that still is sweet.
But the flower-fed buffaloes of the spring
Left us, long ago.
They gore no more, they bellow no more,
They trundle around the hills no more:—
With the Blackfeet, lying low,
With the Pawnees, lying low,
Lying low.

II. BALLADS, WRECKS,

BLUES, AND HOBOES

I been ridin' them fast rattlers, I thought you knowed;
I been ridin' them flat wheelers, way down the road.
I been ridin' them dead enders, blind passengers, pickin' up cinders—
I been havin' some hard travelin', Lord.
—Woody Guthrie, from "Hard Travelin'"

STERLING A. BROWN

CALL BOY

Git out o' bed, you rascals,
Take it up from de covers,
Bring it to de strawboss
Fast as you can;
Down to de railroads
De day is beginnin',
An' day never waited
Fo' no kinda man.

Sun's jes a-peekin'
Over top o' de mountains,
An' de fogclouds a-liftin'
Fo' de break of day;
Number Forty-four's pantin',
Takin' on coal an' water,
An' she's strainin' ready
Fo' to git away.

Leave yo' wives an' yo' sweethearts,
Yo' pink and yo' yaller,
Yo' blue black and stovepipe,
Yo' chocolate brown;
All you backbitin' rascals,
Leave de other men's women,
De night crew from de roundhouse
Is a-roundin' roun'.

O you shifters and humpers,
You boiler washers,
You oilers and you greasers

Of de drivin' rods,
You switchers and flagmen,
Tile layers and tampers,
Youse wanted at de Norfolk
And Western yards.

You cooks got to cook it
From here to Norfolk,
You waiters got to dish it
From here to Tennessee,
You porters got to run
From here to Memphis,
Gotta bring de man's time,
Dontcha see, dontcha see?

De air may be cold, an'
Yo' bed may be easy,
Yo' babe may be comfy
An' warm by yo' side;
But don't snore so loud
Dat you can't hear me callin',
Don't ride no nightmare,
Dere's engines to ride.

Git up off o' yo shirt-tails,
You dumb lazy rounders,
Think I'm gonna let you
Sleep all day?
Bed has done ruint
Dem as can't leave it,
You knows you can't make it
Actin' datway. . . .

T. LAWRENCE SEIBERT

CASEY JONES

Come all ye rounders, for I want you to hear,
The story of a brave engineer.
Casey Jones was the rounder's name.
On a big eight wheeler of a mighty fame.

Caller called Casey 'bout half-past four,
He kissed his wife at the station door,
Climbed to the cab with the orders in his hand,
He says, "This is my trip to the holy land."

Out of South Memphis yard on the fly,
Heard the fireman say, "You got a white eye."
Well, the switchmen knew by the engine moan
That the man at the throttle was Casey Jones.

The rain was comin' down five or six weeks.
The railroad track was like the bed of a creek.
They slowed her down to a thirty mile gait
And the south-bound mail was eight hours late.

Fireman says, "Casey, you're runnin' too fast,
You run that block board the last station you passed."
Casey says, "I believe we'll make it though,
For she steams a lot better than I ever know."

Casey says, "Fireman, don't you fret,
Keep knockin' at the fire door, don't give up yet,
I'm going to run her till she leaves the rail,
Or make it on time with the south-bound mail."

Around the curve and down the dump,
Two locomotives was a bound to jump,
Fireman hollered, "Casey, it's just ahead,
We might jump and make it but we'll all be dead."

Around the curve comes a passenger train,
Casey blows the whistle, tells the fireman, "Ring the bell,"
Fireman jumps and says "Good-by,
Casey Jones, You're bound to die."

Well Casey Jones was all right.
He stuck to his duty day and night.
They loved his whistle and his ring number three,
And he came into Memphis on the old I. C.

Fireman goes down the depot track,
Begging his honey to take him back,
She says, "Oranges on the table, peaches on the shelf,
You're a goin' to get tired sleepin' by yourself."

Mrs. Casey Jones was a sittin' on the bed.
Telegram comes that Casey is dead.
She says, "Children, go to bed, and hush your cryin',
'Cause you got another papa on the Frisco line."

Headaches and heartaches and all kinds of pain.
They ain't apart from a railroad train.
Stories of brave men, noble and grand,
Belong to the life of a railroad man.

DAVID GRAVES GEORGE

WRECK OF THE OLD 97

On a cold frosty morning in the month of September
When the clouds were hanging low,
Ninety-seven pulled out of the Washington station
Like an arrow shot from a bow.

Old Ninety-seven was the fastest mail train
That was ever on the Southern line,
But when she got to Monroe, Virginia
She was forty-seven minutes behind.

Oh, they handed him his orders at Monroe, Virginia,
Saying: "Steve, you're away behind time.
This is not 38, but it's old 97
You must put 'er in Spencer on time."

Steve Broady said to his black greasy fireman,
"Just shovel in a little more coal,
And when we cross the White Oak Mountain
You can watch Old 97 roll."

It's a mighty rough road from Lynchburg to Danville
And the line's on a three mile grade.
It was on that grade that he lost his air brakes
And you see what a jump he made.

He was going down hill at ninety miles an hour
When the whistle broke into a scream—
He was found in the wreck with his hand on the throttle
And scalded to death by the steam.

Now ladies you must all take fair warning
From this time ever more—
Never speak harsh words to your true loving husbands
They may leave you and never return.

T. R. HUMMER

TRAIN WRECK, 1890: MY GRANDMOTHER

LIES DOWN WITH THE DEAD

You come to in the past, dark, where the fires still burn
Hot enough in the wreck of the tender to turn iron
Bright, and that red light hovers over the bodies

Heaped just down the embankment—waking, you
Remember only the dream you were having an hour ago,
Asleep on your father's lap in half-dark, dead

Of morning. What was the dream? The porter
Passes quietly in gas-light, sees the right hand
Of the small girl, draped on the fat man's lap, clench.

The fat man is sleeping too, his head lolled
At a broke-neck angle onto the woman's shoulder.
The woman is awake. She takes your hand,

Unrolls the fingers gently. You were holding on
To something in your dream. The porter smiles
At white people's human love, thinks of his own

Granddaughter, tips his cap, goes down
The aisle toward the club car he will never come to.
Coming to, you can only open one eye. Above you

On the slope, coal from the tender smokes thick,
And you think you see men running. Where you are
It is quiet, dark, everything is a long way off

But the dream. You jerk
When the porter slams the door. Your mother
Touches your hair, speaks a word, inaudible, her hand

On your face, in love, in your sleep. She is looking
At your black sweep of hair, delicate twitch
Of eyelids: knows you dream, knows you see

What you will never tell her, something shaken
Out of you by the rattle of the coach, the touch
Of the hand you do not wake to. She leans

Over you, squints at your face, traces,
Not touching skin, the line of your jawbone—
It is not in your dream, the distance of breath

Her fingers are from your face. You will not remember
The hard wonder she stares down at you the moment before
Something breaks deep in the line, the dark you come to

Alone, burned in the shadow of smoke and the lap of the dead
Stranger strange men find you next to, men who lift you,
Look hard in your face, lay you down, believing you

Will never open your eyes in this iron-light of the tender,
Never tell them who, in the black plunge of love,
You belong to again.

TRAINWRECKED SOLDIERS

Death, that is small respecter of distinction,
Season or fitness, in an instant these
Tan casual heroes, floral with citation,
Scattered for blocks over the track
In lewd ridiculous poses, red and black.

These had outfaced him in the echoing valleys;
Thwarted like men of stone incredible fire;
Like dancers had evaded the snub bayonet;
Had ridden ocean or precipitous air.
Death turned his face aside, seemed not to see.
His unconcern made boyish melodrama
Of all that sergeant threatened, corporal bore,
Or captain shouted on the withering shore.

He watched the newsreel general pinning on their
Blouses the motley segments of renown;
Stood patient at the cots of wounded
Where metal pruned and comas hung;
Nodded to hear their plans: one with a child
His arms had never held; one with a bride;
One with a mere kid's longing for the gang
In green and ticking poolroom bluff with beer.
All these he herded through sargasso of mines
Back to the native field and Sunday steeple
Where only the russet hunters late in fall
Nitre the frosty heaven with abrupt smoke.
There he arose full height, suddenly spoke.

Spoke, and the four dimensions rocked and shattered;
Rearing, the olive pullmans spun like tops;

Corridors shrank to stairway and shot up;
Window, green pastoral lately, turned grenade;
The very walls were scissor and cut flesh.
Captain and sergeant tumbled, wholly void
Their muscle, fortitude, and khaki fame
Like rules intended for another game.

Then death, the enormous insolence effected,
The tour de force pat and precisely timed,
Resumes his usual idiom, less florid:
A thousand men are broken at Cologne;
Elderly salesman falters on the landing;
Girl Slain in Park; Plane Overdue; Tots Drown.
But we who walk this track, who read, or see
In a dark room the shaggy films of wreck—
What do the carrion bent like letters spell
More than the old *sententiae* of chance?
Greek easier (αἴλινον αἴλινον) than this fact.
You lie wry X, poor men, or empty O,
Crux in a savage tongue none of us know.

ROBERT HEDIN

THE WRECK OF THE GREAT NORTHERN

Where the Great Northern plunged in
The river boiled with light, and we all stood
In the tall grass staring at a tangle
Of track, and four orange coaches

And one Pullman lying under the current,
Turning the current clear. We stood staring
As though it had been there all along
And was suddenly thrust up out of the weeds
That night as a blessing, as a long sleek hallway
Dropping off into fields we'd never seen,
Into the pastures of some great god
Who sent back our steers too heavy to move,
All bloated and with green seaweed strung down
Their horns. And we all looked down
Into the lit cars at businessmen
And wives, already back to breathing water,
And saw in the cold clear tanks of the Pullman
A small child the size of my son, a porter's
White jacket, a nylon floating gracefully
As an eel.
            What the train and the river
Were saying, no one could understand.
We just stood there, breathing what was left
Of the night. How still the cars were,
How sleek, shimmering through the undertow.
And I saw the trees around us blossomed out,
The wind had come back and was blowing
Through the tall empty grass, through the high
Grain fields, the wind was rattling
The dry husks of corn.

HAYDEN CARRUTH

THE WRECK OF THE CIRCUS TRAIN

Couplings buckled, cracked, collapsed,
And all reared, wheels and steel
Pawing and leaping above the plain,

And fell down totally, a crash
Deep in the rising surf of dust,
As temples into their cellars crash.

Dust flattened across the silence
That follows the end of anything,
Drifted into cracks of wreckage.

But motion remained, a girder
Found gravity and shifted, a wheel
Turned lazily, turning, turning,

And life remained, at work to
Detain spirit: three lions, one
Male with wide masculine mane,

Two female, short, strong, emerged
And looked quickly over the ruin,
Turned and moved toward the hills.

BLIND LEMON JEFFERSON

EASY RIDER BLUES

Now tell me where my easy rider gone
Tell me where my easy rider gone
I need one of these women always in the wrong

Well, easy rider, standing on the road
And it's easy rider standing on the road
I'm a poor blind man, ain't got no where to go

It's gonna be the time when a woman don't need no man
Well, it's gonna be a time when a woman don't need no man
Then, baby, shut your mouth: it's gonna be raising sand

The train I ride don't burn no coal at all
Train I ride don't burn no coal at all
The coal house burner: everybody's snapping cannonballs

I went to the depot
I mean I went to the depot and set my pistol down
The blues overtake me and tears come rolling down

The woman I love, she must be out of town
Woman I love, man she's out of town
She left me this morning with a face that's travel bound

I got a gal 'cross town, she crochets all the time
I got a gal 'cross town, crochets all the time
Baby, if you don't quit crocheting, you gonna lose your mind

Goodbye brown, what's the matter now
Goodbye brown, what's the matter now
You turn your back to quit me: woman, and you don't know how

BILL MONROE

IN THE PINES

The longest train I ever saw
Went down that Georgia line
The engine passed at 6 o'clock
The cab passed by at 9.

In the pines, in the pines, where the sun never shines
And we shiver when the cold wind blows.

I asked my captain for the time of day
He said he throwed his watch away
A long steel rail and a short crosstie
I'm on my way back home.

Little girl, little girl, what have I done
That makes you treat me so?
You caused me to weep, you caused me to moan
You caused me to leave my home.

BIG BILL BROONZY

THE SOUTHERN BLUES

When I got up this mornin', I heard the old Southern whistle blow,
When I got up this mornin', I heard the old Southern whistle blow.
Then I was thinkin' 'bout my baby, Lord, I sure did want to go.

I was standin', lookin' and listenin', watchin' the Southern cross
    the Dog,
I was standin', lookin' and listenin', watchin' the Southern cross
    the Dog.
If my baby didn't catch that Southern, she must have caught that
    Yellow Dog.

Down at the station, looked up on the board, waitin' for the conductor
    just to say, "All aboard,"
Down at the station, Lord, I looked up on the board,
I don't know my baby left from here, ooh, but I was told.

I'm goin' to Moorhead, get me a job on the Southern line,
Said I'm goin' to Moorhead, get me a job on the Southern line;
So that I can make some money just to send for that brown of mine.

The Southern crossed the Dog in Moorhead, my my Lord, and she
    keeps on through,
The Southern crossed the Dog in Moorhead, my my Lord, and she
    keeps on through.
I say my baby's gone to Georgia, I believe I'll go to Georgia, too.

STERLING A. BROWN

LONG TRACK BLUES

Went down to the yards
To see the signal lights come on;
Looked down the track
Where my lovin' babe done gone.

Red light in my block,
Green light down the line;
Lawdy, let yo' green light
Shine down on that babe o' mine.

Heard a train callin'
Blowin' long ways down the track;
Ain't no train due here,
Baby, what can bring you back?

Brakeman tell me
Got a powerful ways to go;
He don't know my feelin's
Baby, when he's talkin' so.

Lanterns a-swingin',
An' a long freight leaves the yard;
Leaves me here, baby,
But my heart it rides de rod.

Sparks a flyin',
Wheels rumblin' wid a mighty roar;
Then the red tail light,
And the place gets dark once more.

Dog in the freight room
Howlin' like he los' his mind;
Might howl myself,
If I was the howlin' kind.

Norfolk and Western,
Baby, and the C. & O.;
How come they treat
A hardluck feller so?

Red light in my block,
Green light down the line;
Lawdy, let yo' green light
Shine down on that babe o' mine.

LANGSTON HUGHES

HOMESICK BLUES

De railroad bridge's
A sad song in de air.
De railroad bridge's
A sad song in de air.
Ever time de trains pass
I wants to go somewhere.

I went down to de station.
Ma heart was in ma mouth.
Went down to de station.

Heart was in ma mouth.
Lookin' for a box car
To roll me to de South.

Homesick blues, Lawd,
'S a terrible thing to have.
Homesick blues is
A terrible thing to have.
To keep from cryin'
I opens ma mouth an' laughs.

ANONYMOUS

THE RAILROAD BLUES

Every time you hear me sing this song
You may know I've caught a train and gone.
I get a letter, and this is how it read:
Stamped on the inside, "Yo' lover's sick in bed."

Give me my shoes and my Carhart overalls,
Let me step over yonder and blind the Cannon Ball;
That's the long train they call the Cannon Ball,
It makes a hundred miles and do no switchin' at all.

Train I ride doan burn no coal at all,
It doan burn nothin' but Texas Beaumont oil;
That's the long train they calls the Cannon Ball,
It makes a hundred miles and do no stoppin' at all.

If you ever had the blues, you know jus' how I feel,
Puts you on the wonder, and make you want to squeal;
When you take the blues and doan know what to do,
Jus' hunt you a train and ride the whole world through.

Big Four in Dallas done burned down,
Burned all night long, burned clean to the ground;
But give me my shoes, and press my overalls,
If you doan min' my goin', baby, I'll catch the Cannon Ball.

I'm worried now, but I won't be worried long,
This north-bound train will certainly take me home.
Number Nine is gone, Number Ten's switchin' in the yard,
But I'm goin' to see that girl if I have to ride the rods.

I got the railroad blues, but I haven't got the fare,
The company sho' ought to pay my way back there.
The train I ride is sixteen coaches long,
Dat's de train done take yo' baby home.

I'm a goin' away, it won't be long;
When I hit Houston, I'll call it gone.
When I git to Houston I'll stop and dry,
When I hit San Tone, I'll keep on by.

How I hate to hear the Monkey Motion blow,
It puts me on the wonder, and makes me want to go.
Dat passenger-train got ways jus' lak a man,
Steal away yo' girl, and doan care where she land.

I may be right an' I may be wrong,
But it takes a worried woman to sing a worry song;
When a woman's in trouble, she wring her hands and cry,
But when a man's in trouble, it's a long freight-train and ride.

DAVID WOJAHN

"MYSTERY TRAIN": JANIS JOPLIN LEAVES

PORT ARTHUR FOR POINTS WEST, 1964

Train she rides is sixteen coaches long,
    The long dark train that takes the girl away.
The silver wheels
                    click and sing along

    The panhandle, the half-assed cattle towns,
All night until the misty break of day.
    Dark train,
                    dark train, sixteen coaches long.

Girl's looked out her window all night long,
    Bad dreams:
                    couldn't sleep her thoughts away.
The wheels click, mournful, dream along.

    Amarillo, Paradise,
                    Albuquerque still a long
Night's ride. Scrub pine, cactus, fog all gray
    Around the dark train
                    sixteen coaches long.

A cardboard suitcase and she's dressed all wrong.
    Got some cousin's address,
                    no skills, no smarts, no money.
The wheels mock her as they click along.

⟨45⟩

A half-pint of Four Roses,
                              then she hums a Woody song,
     "I Ain't Got No Home."
                              The whistle brays.
The Mystery Train is sixteen coaches long.

     The whistle howls, the wheels click along.

ANONYMOUS
─────────────

RAILROAD BILL
─────────────

Railroad Bill, Railroad Bill,
He never work and he never will;
Well, it's bad Railroad Bill.

Railroad Bill, Railroad Bill,
Took ev'thing that the farmer had;
That bad Railroad Bill.

Railroad Bill had no wife,
Always looking for somebody's wife;
Then it's ride, ride, ride.

Kill me a chicken, send me the wing,
They think I'm working but I ain't done a thing;
Then it's ride, ride, ride.

Railroad Bill, mighty bad man,
Shoot the lantern out the brakeman's han',
Bad Railroad Bill.

⟨ 46 ⟩

Railroad Bill, desp'rate an' bad,
Take ev'thing po' women's had;
Then it's ride, ride, ride.

Railroad Bill, coming home soon,
Killed MacMillan by the light o' the moon;
Then it's ride, ride, ride.

MacMillan had a special train,
When he got there it was spring,
Well, it's ride, ride, ride.

Two policemen, dressed in blue,
Come down the street in two and two;
Well, it's looking for Railroad Bill.

Ev'body tol' him he better turn back,
Bill was a-going down the railroad track;
Well it's ride, ride, ride.

ROBERT PENN WARREN

BALLAD: BETWEEN THE BOXCARS

I. I CAN'T EVEN REMEMBER THE NAME

I can't even remember the name of the one who fell
Flat on his ass, on the cinders, between the boxcars.
I can't even remember whether he got off his yell
Before what happened had happened between the boxcars.

But whether or not he managed to get off his yell,
I remember its shape on his mouth, between the boxcars,
And it was the shape that yours would be too if you fell
Flat on your ass, on the cinders, between the boxcars.

And there's one sure thing you had better remember well,
You go for the grip at the front, not the back, of the boxcars.
Miss the front, you're knocked off—miss the back, you never can tell
But you're flat on your ass, on the cinders, between the boxcars.

He was fifteen and old enough to know perfectly well
You go for the grip at the front, not the back, of the boxcars,
But he was the kind of smart aleck you always can tell
Will end flat on his ass, on the cinders, between the boxcars.

Suppose I remembered his name, then what the hell
Good would it do him now between the boxcars?
But it might mean something to me if I could tell
You the name of the one who fell between the boxcars.

II. HE WAS FORMIDABLE

He was formidable, he was, the little booger,
As he spat in his hands and picked up the Louisville Slugger,
And at that bat-crack
Around those bases he could sure ball the jack,
And if from the outfield the peg had beat him home,
He would slide in slick, like a knife in a nigger.
So we dreamed of an afternoon to come,
In the Series, the ninth-inning hush, in the Yankee Stadium,
Sun low, score tied, bases full, two out, and he'd waltz to the
    plate with his grin—
But no, oh no, not now, not ever! for in
That umpireless rhubarb and steel-heeled hugger-mugger,
    He got spiked sliding home, got spiked between the boxcars.

Oh, his hair was brown-bright as a chestnut, sun-glinting and curly,
And that lip that smiled boy-sweet could go, of a sudden, man-surly,

⟨ 48 ⟩

And the way he was built
Made the girls in his grade stare in darkness, and finger the quilt.
Yes, he was the kind you know born to give many delight,
And entering on such life-labor early,
Would have moved, bemused, in that rhythm and rite,
Through blood-throbbing blackness and moon-gleam and pearly
    thigh-glimmer of night,
To the exquisite glut: *Woman Slays Self for Love*, as the tabloids
    would tell—
But no, never now! Like a kid in his first brothel,
In that hot clasp and loveless hurly-burly,
    He spilled, as boys may, too soon, between the boxcars.

Or, he might have managed the best supermarket in town,
Bright with banners and chrome, where housewives push carts up
    and down,
And morning and night
Walked the street with his credit *A*-rated and blood pressure right,
His boy a dentist in Nashville, his girl at State Normal;
Or a scientist flushed with *Time*-cover renown
For vaccine, or bomb, or smog removal;
Or a hero with phiz like hewn cedar, though young for the stars of
    a general,
Descending the steps of his personal plane to view the home-town
    unveiling.
But no, never now!—battle-cunning, the test tube, retailing,
All, all, in a helter-skeltering mishmash thrown
    To that clobber and grind, too soon, between the boxcars.

But what is success, or failure, at the last?
The newspaper whirled down the track when the through freight
    has passed
Will sink from that gust
To be of such value as it intrinsically must,
And why should we grieve for the name that boy might have made
To be printed on newsprint like that, for that blast
To whirl with the wheels' fanfaronade,
When we cannot even remember his name, nor humbly have prayed
That when that blunt grossness, slam-banging, bang-slamming,

blots black the last blue flash of sky,
And our own lips utter the crazed organism's cry,
We may know the poor self not alone, but with all who are cast
To that clobber, and slobber, and scream, between the boxcars?

JAMES DICKEY

A FOLK SINGER OF THE THIRTIES

On a bed of gravel moving
Over the other gravel
Roadbed between the rails, I lay
As in my apartment now.
I felt the engine enter
A tunnel a half-mile away
And settled deeper
Into the stones of my sleep
Drifting through North Dakota.
I pulled them over me
For warmth, though it was summer,
And in the dark we pulled

Into the freight yards of Bismarck.
In the gravel car buried
To my nose in sledge-hammered stones,
My guitar beside me straining
Its breast beneath the rock,
I lay in the buzzing yards
And crimson hands swinging lights

Saw my closed eyes burn
Open and shine in their lanterns.
The yard bulls pulled me out,
Raining a rockslide of pebbles.
Bashed in the head, I lay

On the ground
As in my apartment now.
I spat out my teeth
Like corn, as they jerked me upright
To be an example for
The boys who would ride the freights
Looking for work, or for
Their American lives.
Four held me stretching against
The chalked red boards,
Spreading my hands and feet,
And nailed me to the boxcar
With twenty-penny nails.
I hung there open-mouthed
As though I had no more weight
Or voice. The train moved out.

Through the landscape I edged
And drifted, my head on my breast
As in my clean sheets now,
And went flying sideways through
The country, the rivers falling
Away beneath my safe
Immovable feet,
Close to me as they fell
Down under the boiling trestles,
And the fields and woods
Unfolded. Sometimes, behind me,
Going into the curves,
Cattle cried in unison,
Singing of stockyards
Where their tilted blood
Would be calmed and spilled.

I heard them until I sailed
Into the dark of the woods,
Flying always into the moonlight
And out again into rain
That filled my mouth
With a great life-giving word,
And into the many lights
The towns hung up for Christmas
Sales, the berries and tinsel,
And then out again
Into the countryside.
Everyone I passed

Could never believe what they saw,
But gave me one look
They would never forget, as I stood
In my overalls, stretched on the nails,
And went by, or stood
In the steaming night yards,
Waiting to couple on,
Overhanging the cattle coming
Into the cars from the night-lights.
The worst pain was when
We shuddered away from the platforms.
I lifted my head and croaked
Like a crow, and the nails
Vibrated with something like music
Endlessly clicking with movement
And the powerful, simple curves.
I learned where the oil lay
Under the fields,
Where the water ran
With the most industrial power,
Where the best corn would grow
And what manure to use
On any field that I saw.
If riches were there,
Whatever it was would light up
Like a bonfire seen through an eyelid

And begin to be words
That would go with the sound of the rails.
Ghostly bridges sprang up across rivers,
Mills towered where they would be,
Slums tottered, and buildings longed
To bear up their offices.
I hung for years
And in the end knew it all
Through pain: the land,
The future of profits and commerce
And also humility
Without which none of it mattered.
In the stockyards west of Chicago

One evening, the orphans assembled
Like choir boys
And drew the nails from my hands
And from my accustomed feet.
I stumbled with them to their homes
In Hooverville

And began to speak
In a chapel of galvanized tin
Of what one wishes for
When streaming alone into woods
And out into sunlight and moonlight
And when having a station lamp bulb
In one eye and not the other
And under the bites
Of snowflakes and clouds of flies
And the squandered dust of the prairies
That will not settle back
Beneath the crops.
In my head the farms
And industrial sites were burning
To produce.
One night, I addressed the A.A.,
Almost singing,
And in the fiery,

Unconsummated desire
For drink that rose around me
From those mild-mannered men,
I mentioned a place for a shoe store
That I had seen near the yards
As a blackened hulk with potential.
A man rose up,
Took a drink from a secret bottle,
And hurried out of the room.
A year later to the day
He knelt at my feet
In a silver suit of raw silk.
I sang to industrial groups
With a pearl-inlaid guitar

And plucked the breast-straining strings
With a nail that had stood through my hand.
I could not keep silent
About the powers of water,
Or where the coal beds lay quaking,
Or where electrical force
Should stalk in its roofless halls
Alone through the night wood,
Where the bridges should leap,
Striving with all their might
To connect with the other shore
To carry the salesmen.
I gave all I knew
To the owners, and they went to work.
I waked, not buried in pebbles

Behind the tank car,
But in the glimmering steeple
That sprang as I said it would
And lifted the young married couples,
Clutching their credit cards,
Boldly into and out of
Their American lives.
I said to myself that the poor

Would always be poor until
The towers I knew of should rise
And the oil be tapped:
That I had literally sung
My sick country up from its deathbed,
But nothing would do,
No logical right holds the truth.
In the sealed rooms I think of this,
Recording the nursery songs
In a checkered and tailored shirt,
As a guest on TV shows
And in my apartment now:
This is all a thing I began
To believe, to change, and to sell
When I opened my mouth to the rich.

THE DELMORE BROTHERS

THE WABASH CANNONBALL

From the rocky-bound Atlantic to the south Pacific shore,
From the coast of Maryland to the ice-bound Labrador;
There's a train of splendor and it's quite well known to all,
The modern 'commodation called the *Wabash Cannonball*.

Great cities of importance, they we reach upon our way,
Chicago and Saint Louis, Rock Island so they say;
Springfield and Decatur, Peoria and them all,
We reach them by no other than the *Wabash Cannonball*.

You can hear the merry jingle and the rumble and the roar,
As she dashes through the woodland, comes creeping 'long the shore;
We hear the engine's whistle and the merry hoboes call,
As they ride the rods and brake-beams on the *Wabash Cannonball*.

There are other cities, partner, as you can easily see,
Saint Paul and Minneapolis and the famous Albert Lea;
The lakes of Minnehaha where the laughing waters fall,
We reach them by no other than the *Wabash Cannonball*.

Now here's to Daddy Claxton, may his name forever stand,
He's a brakeman that's respected by the hoboes in the land;
And when his days are over and the curtains round him fall,
May his spirit ever linger on the *Wabash Cannonball*.

You can hear the merry jingle and the rumble and the roar,
As she dashes through the woodland, comes creeping 'long the shore;
We hear the engine's whistle and the merry hoboes call,
As they ride the rods and brake-beams on the *Wabash Cannonball*.

ANONYMOUS

———————————

HALLELUJAH, BUM AGAIN

———————————————

1

Oh, why don't I work like the other men do?
How the hell can I work when the skies are so blue?

Chorus:
Hallelujah, I'm a bum!
Hallelujah, bum again,
Hallelujah! Bum a handout,
Revive me again.

If I was to work and save all I earn,
I could buy me a bar and have whiskey to burn.

Oh, I love Jim Hill, he's an old friend of mine,
Up North I ride rattlers all over his line.

Oh, I ride box cars and I ride fast mails,
When it's cold in the winter I sleep in the jails.

I passed by a saloon and I hear someone snore,
And I found the bartender asleep on the floor.

I stayed there and drank till a fly-mug came in,
And he put me to sleep with a sap on the chin.

Next morning in court I was still in a haze,
When the judge looked at me, he said, "Thirty days!"

Some day a long train will run over my head,
And the sawbones will say, "Old One-Finger's dead!"

2

When springtime does come,
Oh, won't we have fun!
We'll all throw up our jobs
And we'll go on the bum.

Chorus:
Hallelujah, I'm a bum,
Hallelujah, bum again,

Hallelujah, give us a handout
To revive us again.

Oh, springtime has come,
And I'm just out of jail,
Ain't got no money,
It all went for bail.

I went up to a house
And I knocked on the door,
A lady came out, says,
"You been here before!"

I went up to a house,
Asked for some bread;
A lady came out, says,
"The baker is dead."

ANONYMOUS

THE BIG ROCK CANDY MOUNTAINS

Introduction:
On a summer day in the month of May,
A burly little bum come a-hikin',
He was travelin' down that lonesome road,
A-lookin' for his likin'.
He was headed for a land that's far away,
Beside those crystal fountains,

"I'll see you all, this comin' fall,
In the Big Rock Candy Mountains."

In the Big Rock Candy Mountains,
You never change your socks,
And the little streams of alkyhol,
Come a-tricklin' down the rocks.
Where the shacks all have to tip their hats,
And the railroad bulls are blind,
There's a lake of stew, and whiskey, too,
In the Big Rock Candy Mountains.

> *Chorus:*
> Oh . . . the . . . buzzin' of the bees
> In the cigarette trees,
> Round the sodawater fountains,
> Now the lemonade springs,
> Where the whangdoodle sings
> In the Big Rock Candy Mountains.

In the Big Rock Candy Mountains,
There's a land that's fair and bright,
Where the handouts grow on bushes,
And you sleep out every night.
Where the boxcars are all empty,
And the sun shines every day,
Oh, I'm bound to go, where there ain't no snow,
Where the rain don't fall and the wind don't blow,
In the Big Rock Candy Mountains.

In the Big Rock Candy Mountains,
The jails are made of tin,
And you can bust right out again,
As soon as they put you in.
The farmers' trees are full of fruit,
The barns are full of hay,
I'm goin' to stay where you sleep all day,
Where they boiled in oil the inventor of toil,
In the Big Rock Candy Mountains.

L. E. SISSMAN

THE BIG ROCK-CANDY MOUNTAIN

To the memory of my half brother, Winfield Shannon,
itinerant farm worker, 1909–1969

A mason times his mallet
to a lark's twitter . . .
till the stone spells a name
naming none,
a man abolished.
—Basil Bunting

I. "ON A SUMMER'S DAY IN THE MONTH OF MAY,
   A JOCKER CAME A-HIKING
   DOWN A SHADY LANE IN THE SUGAR CANE,
   A-LOOKING FOR HIS LIKING. . . ."

The land was theirs after we were the land's,
The visionaries with prehensile hands—
The Wobblies, Okies, wetbacks—driven and drawn
To cross the land and see it, to select
A tree to lie out under: a Pound Sweet,
A Cox's Orange Pippin, a pecan,
Persimmon, Bartlett, quince, Bing, freestone, fig,
Grapefruit, Valencia. The trundling trains
That took their supercargo free are gone,
And so are they; a thousand circling camps
Down by the freight yards are dispersed, watchfires
Burnt out, inhabitants transshipped
To death or terminal respectability
In cold wards of the state, where their last rites
Are levied on the people, ritual
Gravediggers of the past, ratepayers for
A lot in potter's field. Old Gravensteins,

⟨ 60 ⟩

Bedight with morbid branches, shelter no
Transients at length. Our suburbs saw them go.

II. "AS HE ROAMED ALONG, HE SANG A SONG
   OF THE LAND OF MILK AND HONEY,
   WHERE A BUM CAN STAY FOR MANY A DAY
   AND HE WON'T NEED ANY MONEY. . . ."

Uninterest in progress was their crime,
Short-circuited ambition. They came out
On a Traverse County hilltop one late-May
Morning and gave an involuntary shout
At those square miles of cherry blossom on
The slopes above the lake; exclaimed at wheat
Fat in the ear and staggered in the wind,
In Hillsdale County; up in Washtenaw,
Spoke to the plough mules and the meadowlark
A little after dawn; in Lenawee,
Laughed at a foal's first grounding in the art
Of standing in the grass. Too tentative,
Too deferent to put down roots beside
Us in our towns, outcast, outcaste, they rode
Out of our sight into the sheltering storm
Of their irrelevant reality:
Those leagues of fields out there beyond the pale
Fretting of cities, where, in prison clothes,
We cultivate our gardens for the rose
Of self redoubled, for the florid green
Of money succulent as cabbage leaves.
They have gone out to pasture. No one grieves.

III. "OH, THE BUZZING OF THE BEES IN THE CIGARETTE TREES,
    THE SODA-WATER FOUNTAIN,
    THE LEMONADE SPRINGS WHERE THE BLUEBIRD SINGS
    ON THE BIG ROCK-CANDY MOUNTAIN. . . ."

A young man on a Harley-Davidson
(An old one painted olive drab, with long-
Horn handlebars and a slab-sided tank),
You pushed your blond hair back one-handed when
You stopped and lit a Camel cigarette.
You laughed and showed white teeth; you had a blond
Mustache; wore cardigans and knickerbockers; wowed
The farm-town girls; drank beer; drew gracefully;
Fell, frothing at the mouth, in a grand mal
Seizure from time to time. In your small room
In Grandpa's house, you kept your goods: pastels,
A sketching block, a superheterodyne
Kit radio, a tin can full of parts,
A stack of *Popular Mechanics*, three
Kaywoodie pipes, an old Antonio
Y Cleopatra box for letters and
Receipts, a Rexall calendar with fat
Full moons controlling 1933.

IV. "OH, THE FARMER AND HIS SON, THEY WERE ON THE RUN,
    TO THE HAYFIELD THEY WERE BOUNDING.
    SAID THE BUM TO THE SON, 'WHY DON'T YOU COME
    TO THAT BIG ROCK-CANDY MOUNTAIN?' . . .

When Grandpa died and your employer died,
And the widow sold off his tax-loss horse farm
(Those Morgans being auctioned, going meek
To new grooms less deft-handed than you were,
To new frame stables and new riding rings),
You hit the road at fifty and alone
Struck out cross country lamely, too damned old
To keep up with the kids or keep out cold

Except with whiskey, cheap and strong. Too long
You hiked from job to picking job, and when
Snow plastered stubble laths, you holed up in
The Mapes Hotel for winter; did odd jobs
To keep in nips of Richmond Rye; dozed through
The night till spring; fared forward once again
To summer's manufactory, a mill
Of insect tickings on a field of gold,
And fall's great remnant store. Last winter, you
Spent your last winter in a coffining
Dead room on Third Street in Ann Arbor, where
Only the landlady climbed up your stair
And passed your unknocked door in sateen mules.

V. "SO THE VERY NEXT DAY THEY HIKED AWAY;
    THE MILEPOSTS THEY KEPT COUNTING,
    BUT THEY NEVER ARRIVED AT THE LEMONADE TIDE
    ON THE BIG ROCK-CANDY MOUNTAIN. . . ."

In Goebel's Funeral Home, where row on row
Of coffins lie at anchor, burning dark
Hulls—walnut, rosewood—on a light-blue tide
Of broadloom, we select Economy—
Grey fibreglass with a white-rayon shroud
And mainsheets—and stand out into the street,
Becalmed already in the April heat
That conjures greenness out of earthen fields,
Tips black twigs pink on trees, starts habit's sweat
Out of Midwestern brows. In Winfield's room,
A cave of unstirred air kept in the dark
By pinholed shades, we shift his transient
Things in a foredoomed hunt for permanent
Memorials. No photograph, no ring,
No watch, no diary, no effects. Nothing—
Beyond a mildewed pile of mackinaws
(On top) and boots (precipitated out)—
Except the lone cigar box. On its lid

A rampant Antony advances on
Bare-breasted Cleopatra, areoles
Red as lit panatelas, but inside,
Only a heap of fingered rent receipts,
On pale-green check stock, weights a linen pad
Of Woolworth letter paper. Here begins
Winfield's last letter, in a corn-grain-round,
School-Palmer-Method hand riven by age,
Drink, sickness: "April 17. Dear Folks—
The weather has warmed up some but I don't"
No more. The hospital bed intervened.
Peritonitis. Coma. Peaceful death.
In truth it is. In Goebel's viewing room
The guest has been laid out, now neat, now dressed—
In shirt, tie, jacket—as if for a feast.
It is not over-stressed. He looks his age
(Not brotherly at all; avuncular,
Judicious, a thought sallow, robbed of the
Brilliance of his two straight and sky-blue eyes)
And takes his silent part upon the stage
Miming repose, an unemotional
Exit dictated by the prompter's page.
Later, in the three-car processional
To the old graveyard, we ride just behind
His Stygian Superior hearse, a Cadillac.
The grave has been dug under tamaracks;
The young Episcopalian minister
Dispassionately, as he should for one unknown
To him, says the set words designed to send
The dead off; soon the open grave will close,
The mason test his chisel and begin,
Tabula rasa, to cut that name in-
To his blank slab of granite, much as that
Void grave will take the imprint of his weight,
And all his travels will be at an end.

ENVOY

But, prince that fortune turned into a toad,
Instead I see you—camped beside a road
Between old fruit trees in full bloom in May—
Lie out under an agèd Pound Sweet and
Sleep soundly on the last night of your way
Out of a rifled and abandoned land.

III. THE FREEDOM TRAIN

Ho the car Emancipation,
Rides majestic thro' our Nation
Bearing on its train the story,
Liberty, a Nation's glory.
—Jesse Hutchinson, "Get off the Tracks"

ROBERT HAYDEN

RUNAGATE RUNAGATE

1

Runs falls rises stumbles on from darkness into darkness
and the darkness thicketed with shapes of terror
and the hunters pursuing and the hounds pursuing
and the night cold and the night long and the river
to cross and the jack-muh-lanterns beckoning beckoning
and blackness ahead and when shall I reach that somewhere
morning and keep on going and never turn back and keep on going

    Runagate
          Runagate
               Runagate

Many thousands rise and go
many thousands crossing over
                    O mythic North
           O star-shaped yonder Bible city

Some go weeping and some rejoicing
some in coffins and some in carriages
some in silks and some in shackles

       Rise and go or fare you well

No more auction block for me
no more driver's lash for me

   If you see my Pompey, 30 yrs of age,
   new breeches, plain stockings, negro shoes;

if you see my Anna, likely young mulatto
branded E on the right cheek, R on the left,
catch them if you can and notify subscriber.
Catch them if you can, but it won't be easy.
They'll dart underground when you try to catch them,
plunge into quicksand, whirlpools, mazes,
turn into scorpions when you try to catch them.

And before I'll be a slave
I'll be buried in my grave

    North star and bonanza gold
    I'm bound for the freedom, freedom-bound
    and oh Susyanna don't you cry for me

        Runagate

        Runagate

2

Rises from their anguish and their power,
                Harriet Tubman,

                      woman of earth, whipscarred,
                      a summoning, a shining

                      Mean to be free

And this was the way of it, brethren brethren,
way we journeyed from Can't to Can.
Moon so bright and no place to hide,
the cry up and the patterollers riding,
hound dogs belling in bladed air.
And fear starts a-murbling, Never make it,
we'll never make it. *Hush that now,*
and she's turned upon us, levelled pistol
glinting in the moonlight:

Dead folks can't jaybird-talk, she says;
you keep on going now or die, she says.

Wanted   Harriet Tubman   alias The General
alias Moses   Stealer of Slaves

In league with Garrison   Alcott   Emerson
Garrett   Douglass   Thoreau   John Brown

Armed and known to be Dangerous

Wanted   Reward   Dead or Alive

    Tell me, Ezekiel, oh tell me do you see
    mailed Jehovah coming to deliver me?

Hoot-owl calling in the ghosted air,
five times calling to the hants in the air.
Shadow of a face in the scary leaves,
shadow of a voice in the talking leaves:

    Come ride-a my train

    Oh that train, ghost-story train
    through swamp and savanna movering movering,
    over trestles of dew, through caves of the wish,
    Midnight Special on a sabre track movering movering,
    first stop Mercy and the last Hallelujah.

    Come ride-a my train

    Mean mean mean to be free.

THE SOUTHERN ROAD

There the black river, boundary to hell.
And here the iron bridge, the ancient car,
And grim conductor, who with surly yell
Forbids white soldiers where the black ones are.
And I re-live the enforced avatar
Of desperate journey to a dark abode
Made by my sires before another war;
And I set forth upon the southern road.

To a land where shadowed songs like flowers swell
And where the earth is scarlet as a scar
Friezed by the bleeding lash that fell (O fell)
Upon my fathers' flesh. O far, far, far
and deep my blood has drenched it. None can bar
My birthright to the loveliness bestowed
Upon this country haughty as a star.
And I set forth upon the southern road.

This darkness and these mountains loom a spell
Of peak-roofed town where yearning steeples soar
And the holy holy chanting of a bell
Shakes human incense on the throbbing air
Where bonfires blaze and quivering bodies char.
Whose is the hair that crisped, and fiercely glowed?
I know it; and my entrails melt like tar
And I set forth upon the southern road.

O fertile hillsides where my fathers are,
From which my griefs like troubled streams have flowed,
I have to love you, though they sweep me far.
And I set forth upon the southern road.

PHILIP BOOTH

STATIONS

The old, their big shoulders humped,
empty grain sacks under each eye,
sit without talk in the waiting room.
In weekly for shots, I've learned to
tell them apart: the doctors who wear
white jackets, old women in discount
dresses, the men with dark pants on.

I guess they must all be dead now:
the Negroes I used to watch back in '44,
each one safe between oak armrests in
an oak pew, waiting for trains or
relatives to arrive, or maybe the war
to end, the far side of the Macon station.

LANGSTON HUGHES

PORTER

I must say
Yes, sir,
To you all the time.
Yes, sir!
Yes, sir!
All my days
Climbing up a great big mountain
Of yes, sirs!

Rich old white man
Owns the world.
Gimme yo' shoes
To shine.

Yes, sir!

LANGSTON HUGHES

JIM CROW CAR

Get out the lunch-box of your dreams.
Bite into the sandwich of your heart,
And ride the Jim Crow car until it screams
Then—like an atom bomb—it bursts apart.

LANGSTON HUGHES

FREEDOM TRAIN

I read in the papers about the
    Freedom Train.
I heard on the radio about the
    Freedom Train.
I seen folks talkin' about the
    Freedom Train.
Lord, I been a-waitin' for the
    Freedom Train!

Down South in Dixie only train I see's
Got a Jim Crow car set aside for me.

I hope there ain't no Jim Crow on the Freedom Train,
No back door entrance to the Freedom Train,
No signs FOR COLORED on the Freedom Train,
No WHITE FOLKS ONLY on the Freedom Train.

    I'm gonna check up on this
       Freedom Train.

Who's the engineer on the Freedom Train?
Can a coal black man drive the Freedom Train?
Or am I still a porter on the Freedom Train?
Is there ballot boxes on the Freedom Train?
When it stops in Mississippi will it be made plain
Everybody's got a right to board the Freedom Train?

    Somebody tell me about this
       Freedom Train!

The Birmingham station's marked COLORED and WHITE.
The white folks go left, the colored go right—
They even got a segregated lane.
Is that the way to get aboard the Freedom Train?

    I got to know about this
       Freedom Train!

If my children ask me, *Daddy, Please explain
Why there's Jim Crow stations for the Freedom Train?*
What shall I tell my children? . . . *You* tell me—
'Cause freedom ain't freedom when a man ain't free.

    But maybe they explains it on the
       Freedom Train.

When my grandmother in Atlanta, 83 and black,
Gets in line to see the Freedom,
Will some white man yell, *Get back!
A Negro's got no business on the Freedom Track!*

> Mister, I thought it were the
> Freedom Train!

Her grandson's name was Jimmy. He died at Anzio.
He died for real. It warn't no show.
The freedom that they carryin' on this Freedom Train,
Is it for real—or just a show again?

> Jimmy wants to know about the
> Freedom Train.

Will *his* Freedom Train come zoomin' down the track
Gleamin' in the sunlight for white and black?
Not stoppin' at no stations marked COLORED nor WHITE,
Just stoppin' in the fields in the broad daylight,
Stoppin' in the country in the wide-open air
Where there never was no Jim Crow signs nowhere,

No Welcomin' Committees, nor politicians of note,
No Mayors and such for which colored can't vote,
And nary a sign of a color line—
For the Freedom Train will be yours and mine!

Then maybe from their graves in Anzio
The G.I.'s who fought will say, *We wanted it so!*
Black men and white will say, *Ain't it fine?*
At home they got a train that's yours and mine!

> Then I'll shout, *Glory for the*
> *Freedom Train!*
> I'll holler, *Blow your whistle,*
> *Freedom Train!*
> *Thank God-A-Mighty! Here's the*
> *Freedom Train!*
> *Get on board our Freedom Train!*

ISHMAEL REED

RAILROAD BILL, A CONJURE MAN

A HOODOO SUITE

Railroad Bill, a conjure man
Could change hisself to a tree
He could change hisself to a
Lake, a ram, he could be
What he wanted to be

When a man-hunt came he became
An old slave shouting boss
He went thataway. A toothless
Old slave standing next to a
Hog that laughed as they
Galloped away.
Would laugh as they galloped
Away

Railroad Bill was a conjure man
He could change hisself to a bird
He could change hisself to a brook
A hill he could be what he wanted
To be

One time old Bill changed hisself
To a dog and led a pack on his
Trail. He led the hounds around
And around. And laughed a-wagging
His tail. And laughed
A-wagging his tail

Morris Slater was from Escambia
County, he went to town a-toting
A rifle. When he left that
Day he was bounty.
Morris Slater was Railroad Bill
Morris Slater was Railroad Bill

Railroad Bill was an electrical
Man he could change hisself into
Watts. He could up his voltage
Whenever he pleased
He could, you bet he could
He could, you bet he could

Now look here boy hand over that
Gun, hand over it now not later
I needs my gun said Morris Slater
The man who was Railroad Bill
I'll shoot you dead you SOB
let me be whatever I please
The policeman persisted he just
Wouldn't listen and was buried the
Following eve. Was buried the
Following eve. Many dignitaries
Lots of speech-making.

Railroad Bill was a hunting man
Never had no trouble fetching game
He hid in the forest for those
Few years and lived like a natural
King. Whenever old Bill would
Need a new coat he'd sound out his
Friend the Panther. When Bill got
Tired of living off plants the
Farmers would give him some hens.
In swine-killing time the leavings of
Slaughter. They'd give Bill the
Leavings of slaughter. When he

needed love their fine Corinas
They'd lend old Bill their daughters

Railroad Bill was a conjure man he
Could change hisself to a song. He
Could change hisself to some blues
Some reds he could be what he wanted
To be

E. S. McMillan said he'd get old
Bill or turn in his silver star
Bill told the Sheriff you best
Leave me be said the outlaw from
Tombigbee. Leave me be warned
Bill in 1893

Down in Yellowhammer land
By the humming Chattahoochee
Where the cajun banjo pickers
Strum. In Keego, Volina, and
Astoreth they sing the song of
How come

Bill killed McMillan but wasn't
Willin rather reason than shoot
A villain. Rather reason than
Shoot McMillan

"Railroad Bill was the worst old coon
Killed McMillan by the light of the
Moon
Was lookin for Railroad Bill
Was lookin for Railroad Bill"

Railroad Bill was a gris-gris man
He could change hisself to a mask
A Ziba, a Zulu
A Zambia mask. A Zaramo
Doll as well

⟨ 80 ⟩

One with a necklace on it
A Zaramo doll made of wood

I'm bad, I'm bad said Leonard
McGowin. He'll be in hell and dead he
    Said in 1896
Shot old Bill at Tidmore's store
This was near Atmore that Bill was
    Killed in 1896.
He was buying candy for some children
Procuring sweets for the farmers' kids

Leonard McGowin and R. C. John as
Cowardly as they come. Sneaked up
On Bill while he wasn't lookin.
Ambushed old Railroad Bill
Ambushed the conjure man. Shot him
In the back. Blew his head off.

Well, lawmen came from miles around
All smiles the lawmen came.
They'd finally got rid of
Railroad Bill who could be what
He wanted to be

Wasn't so the old folks claimed
From their shacks in the Wawbeek
Wood. That aint our Bill in that
old coffin, that aint our man
You killed. Our Bill is in the
Dogwood flower and in the grain
We eat
See that livestock grazing there
That Bull is Railroad Bill
The mean one over there near the
Fence, that one is Railroad Bill

Now Hollywood they's doing old
Bill they hired a teacher from

Yale. To treat and script and
Strip old Bill, this classics
Professor from Yale.
He'll take old Bill the conjure
Man and give him a-na-ly-sis. He'll
Put old Bill on a leather couch
And find out why he did it.
Why he stole the caboose and
Avoided nooses why Bill raised so
Much sand.

He'll say Bill had a complex
He'll say it was all due to Bill's
Mother. He'll be playing the
Dozens on Bill, this
Professor from Yale

They'll make old Bill a neurotic
Case these tycoons of the silver
Screen. They'll take their cue
From the teacher from Yale they
Gave the pile of green
A bicycle-riding dude from Yale
Who set Bill for the screen
Who set Bill for the screen

They'll shoot Bill zoom Bill and
Pan old Bill until he looks plain
Sick. Just like they did old Nat
The Fox and tried to do Malik
Just like they did Jack Johnson
Just like they did Jack Johnson

But it wont work what these hacks
Will do, these manicured hacks from
Malibu cause the people will see
That aint our Bill but a haint of
The silver screen. A disembodied
Wish of a Yalie's dream

⟨ 82 ⟩

Our Bill is where the camellia
Grows and by the waterfalls. He's
Sleeping in a hundred trees and in
A hundred skies. That cumulus
That just went by that's Bill's
Old smiling face. He's having a joke
On Hollywood
He's on the varmint's case.

Railroad Bill was a wizard. And
His final trick was tame. Wasn't
Nothing to become some celluloid
And do in all the frames.
Destroy the original copy
Pour chemicals on the master's
Copy

And how did he manage technology
And how did Bill get so modern?
He changed hisself to a production
Assistant and went to work with
The scissors.
While nobody looked he scissored
Old Bill he used the scissors.

Railroad Bill was a conjure man
He could change hisself to the end.
He could outwit the chase and throw
Off the scent he didn't care what
They sent. He didn't give a damn what
They sent.
Railroad Bill was a conjure man
Railroad Bill was a star he could change
Hisself to the sun, the moon
Railroad Bill was free
Railroad Bill was free

THE MIDNIGHT SPECIAL

Well, you wake up in the mornin', hear the ding dong ring,
You go a-marchin' to the table, see the same damn thing.
Well, it's on a one table, knife, a fork, an' a pan,
An' if you say anything about it, you're in trouble with the man.

> *Chorus:*
> Let the Midnight Special shine its light on me,
> Let the Midnight Special shine its ever-lovin' light on me.

If you go to Houston, you better walk right;
You better not stagger, you better not fight,
Or Sheriff Benson will arrest you, he will carry you down.
If the jury finds you guilty, you'll be penitentiary-bound.

Yonder come li'l Rosie. How in the worl' do you know?
I can tell her by her apron and the dress she wo',
Umbrella on her shoulder, piece o' paper in her han'.
Well, I heard her tell the captain: "I want my man."

I'm gwine away to leave you, an' my time ain't long.
The man is gonna call me an' I'm a-goin' home.
Then I'll be done all my grievin', whoopin', holl'in, an' a-cryin',
Then I'll be done all my studyin' 'bout my great long time.

Well, the biscuits on the table, just as hard as any rock.
If you try to swallow them, break a convict's heart.
My sister wrote a letter, my mother wrote a card—
"If you want to come an' see us, you'll have to ride the rods."

JOSEPH BRUCHAC III

LET THE MIDNIGHT SPECIAL

In this year of executioners' songs,
another music stirs my memory,
a part of that time when we
lived in flowered dreams
as Credence sang, rough-voiced
as a southern spring:
Let the Midnight Special
shine its light on me.

Remember the story of how that song
was composed in a prison
where the moonshine beam
of a late freight would cut
across walls
as men held out their hands

knowing that if
that brilliance
touched them
they'd go free.

Today
the tracks
curve further away
and names are buried under stone.

Will their bones
make the mortar stronger
as each mile of the Great Wall
of China, built to keep barbarians out
was reinforced with peasants' blood?

Astronauts say
that of all we have made
that ambling line
of futile stone
is the clearest thing seen
by an eye far out in space.

Its long shadow is clear
as iron rails
touched by moon's reflecting light.

Who is riding
that train tonight?

IV. ASCENDING TIES

E. E. CUMMINGS

(ONE FINE DAY)

let's take the train
for because dear

whispered again
in never's ear
(i'm tho thcared

giggling lithped now
we muthn't pleathe
don't as pop weird
up her hot ow

you hurt tho nithe
steered his big was)
thither to thence
swore many a vow
but both made sense

in when's haymow
with young fore'er
(oh & by the way
asked sis breath
of brud breathe
how is aunt death

did always teethe

KARL SHAPIRO

TERMINAL

Over us stands the broad electric face
With semaphores that flick into the gaps,
Notching the time on sixtieths of space,
Springing the traveller through the folded traps
Downstairs with luggage anywhere to go
While others happily toil upward too;
Well-dressed or stricken, banished or restored,
Hundreds step down and thousands get aboard.

In neat confusion, tickets in our brain
We press the hard plush to our backs and sigh;
The brakeman thumbs his watch, the children strain
The windows to their smeary sight—Goodbye,
The great car creaks, the stone wall turns away
And lights flare past like fishes undersea;
Heads rolling heavily and all as one
With languid screams we charge into the sun.

Now through the maelstrom of the town we ride
Clicking with speed like skates on solid ice;
Streets drop and buildings silently collide,
Rails spread apart, converge and neatly splice.
Through gasping blanks of air we pound and ford
Bulking our courage forward like a road,
Climbing the world on long dead-level stairs
With catwalk stilts and trestles hung by hairs.

Out where the oaks on wide turntables grow
And constellation hamlets gyre and glow,
The straight-up bridges dive and from below

The river's sweet eccentric borders flow;
Into the culverts sliced like lands of meat,
Armies of cornstalks on their ragged feet,
And upward-outward toward the blueback hill
Where clouds of thunder graze and drink their fill.

And always at our side, swifter than we
The racing rabbits of the wire lope
And in their blood the words at liberty
Outspeed themselves; but on our rail we grope
Drinking from one white wire overhead
Hot drinks of action and hell's fiery feed.
Lightly the finger-shaped antennae feel
And lightly cheer the madness of our wheel.

We turn, we turn, thrumming the harp of sounds
And all is pleasure's move, motion of joy;
Now we imagine that we go like hounds
And now like sleds and now like many a toy
Coming alive on Christmas Day to crawl
Between the great world of the floor and wall,
But on the peak of speed we flag and fall—
Fixed on the air we do not move at all.

Arrived at space we settle in our car
And stare like souls admitted to the sky;
Nothing at length is close at hand or far;
All feats of image vanish from the eye.
Upon our brow is set the bursting star,
Upon the void the wheel and axle-bar,
The planetary fragments broken lie;
Distance is dead and light can only die.

CARL SANDBURG

LIMITED

I am riding on a limited express, one of the crack trains of the nation.
Hurtling across the prairie into blue haze and dark air go fifteen
    all-steel coaches holding a thousand people.
(All the coaches shall be scrap and rust and all the men and women
    laughing in the diners and sleepers shall pass to ashes.)
I ask a man in the smoker where he is going and he answers:
    "Omaha."

ROBERT FRANCIS

NIGHT TRAIN

Across the dim frozen fields of night
Where is it going, where is it going?
No throb of wheels, no rush of light,
Only a whistle blowing, blowing,
Only a whistle blowing.

Something echoing through my brain,
Something timed between sleep and waking,

Murmurs, murmurs this may be the train
I must be sometime, somewhere taking,
I must be sometime taking.

ANONYMOUS

THE GOSPEL TRAIN

The gospel train is moving,
   I hear it just at hand;
I hear the carwheel moving,
   And rumbling through the land.

   Chorus:
   Get on board, children,
      Get on board, children,
   Get on board, children,
      For there's room for many more.

I hear the bell and whistle,
   They're coming round the curve;
She's playing all her steam and power,
   And straining every nerve.

O see the gospel engine,
   She's heaving now in sight;
Her steam-valves they are groaning,
   The pressure is so great.

No signal for another train,
    To follow in the line;
O sinner, you're forever lost,
    If once you're left behind.

O see the engine banner,
    She's flut'ring in the breeze;
She's spangled with the Savior's blood,
    But she still floats at ease.

This is the Christian banner,
    The motto's new and old,
Repentance and Salvation
    Are burnished there in gold.

She's nearing on the station;
    O sinners don't be vain,
But come and get your ticket,
    And be ready for the train.

The fare is cheap and all can go,
    The rich and poor are there;
No second class are on board this train,
    No difference in the fare.

We soon shall reach the station,
    O how we then shall sing
With all the heavenly army
    On that celestial shore.

ANONYMOUS

THE BEULAH RAILWAY

God a great railway to heaven has planned,
He staked out the line with His dear, loving hand;
Away back in Eden the grant was first given,
On Calvary's cross the last spike was driven.
The road was surveyed with a special design,
To make it a practical Holiness line;
The grade was thrown up with the greatest of care,
Directly through Canaan, a country most fair.

Of fasting and praying the ballast was made,
The ties are as solid as when they were laid;
The crossings are guarded, not a curve on the track,
Trains never take siding, nor ever turn back.
The streams are all spanned by bridges of Faith,
The last one we cross is the river of Death.

Vestibule coaches, God's chariots they are;
"Holiness to the Lord" is inscribed on each car;
Trains stop at all stations where signal is given,
And run to the Grand Central Depot in Heaven.
Conviction's the station where sinners get in,
Soon reaching Repentance, confessing their sin;
And Faith is the office where tickets are sold
And baggage checked through to the City of Gold.

Regeneration comes next into view.
The heart is now changed and all things become new;
God's spirit bears witness with that of our own,
That we are His children, joint heirs to His throne.
The gauge is quite narrow, with rails from above;

Salvation's the engine, 't is driven by love.
Following the Spirit along in the light,
The old Carnal Nature now comes into sight.
"Inbred Sin" the porter calls out through the train,
"Put off the old man, he cannot remain."

But trusting in Jesus and reading His Word,
The all-cleansing fountain is seen in the Blood;
By faith we step in and its waves o'er us flow,
We rise from the pool and are whiter than snow.
What transports of rapture now sweep o'er the plain.
The music of Paradise filling that train.
Oh ecstasy, ravishing! fountain of bliss!
Scenery celestial! Is Heaven like this?

Jesus, the heavenly Bridegroom, is near,
Making perfect in love and casting out fear;
Our hearts are made younger as onward we glide,
Our strength is renewed, our needs are supplied.
All glory to Jesus! Hallelujah! Praise God!
Travel is luxury on the old Beulah Road,
God's railway celestial encircling the globe;
The good of all ages have travelled this road.
Elijah and Enoch by official request,
Ran in on a special, not stopping at Death.

No accident has this railway yet known,
The Dispatcher is He who sits on the throne.
Trains only move at Jehovah's command,
He holds the throttle with Omnipotent hand.
The Holy Spirit is the headlight so clear,
Revealing the track to the wise engineer.
The angels are brakemen, so kind and urbane,
Adding much to the comfort of all on the train.

Dying Love is a town in the Valley of Fear,
The backslider's repair shops are located here,
Are your vows broken, have you been untrue?
Step into these shops and be burnished anew.

Dear sinners, take passage for Heaven today,
Make haste, there is danger and death in delay.
The Spirit is calling, and so is the Bride;
Our train is now coming, and you must decide.

ANDREW HUDGINS
───────────────────────

THE SOUTHERN CRESCENT WAS ON TIME
───

I played piano while my daddy knelt,
unlaced their shoes, and washed the clean pink feet
they'd washed before they'd come to have them washed.
He never just slopped water on the feet
like some men do. Instead he'd lift each foot,
working the soapy rag between their toes
with such relentless tenderness the boys
would giggle, girls would blush, and women sigh.
And though the feet looked clean to begin with,
when he was done the water was as black
as crankcase oil.
                    And then he'd preach, preach hard.
Black suit, black tie, white shirt gone limp with heat,
he'd slap the pulpit and a spray of sweat
would fly into the air. He'd wipe his brow,
letting the silence work into the crowd,
and then start low, or with—almost—a shout.
I never could guess which. His face would gleam
with sweat. It was as if he were, each night,
baptizing himself from the inside out.

As you drive home tonight, he'd say, *a truck*
a diesel truck,

            might cross into your lane
and you would die apart from God,

                        unsaved.
One night a pair of twins sat in this tent
and each one heard God speaking to his heart.
Come up for God's free cleansing love.

                      Come up.

Let Jesus take your sins away.

                Come up.

They'd come and Daddy would dunk them on the spot
so they could face the family car in peace.
Waiting for them as they lurched down the aisle,
he stood, head bowed, arms raised above his head,
and I would play until his hands came down
and touched his belt. And once I played
twenty-two verses of "Just As I Am"
while Daddy stood there stubbornly, arms raised,
waiting for God to move their hardened hearts.
I prayed that someone would be saved. My sweat
dripped on my hands. My fingers cramped
and skittered on the keys, then I passed out.

            When I came to,
the crowd was gone and Daddy's coat was tucked
beneath my head. He rubbed my arms, rolling
the limp flesh back and forth between his hands.
His eyes were focused past the empty chairs
and out the door. His lips moved silently
so I could tell he was praying for me.
But what, I didn't ask or want to know.

One twin came forward to be saved,

                    and one
stayed in his seat,

              resisted God's free grace.

He needed time to think—or so he thought—
but you can't know when God will take you back.
The earth is not our home. We're passing through.
That night
            as they drove to the Dairy Queen
their brand-new car stalled on the railroad track.
That night
            the Southern Crescent was on time.
One went to heaven with his loving God,
and we know where the other went,
                                    don't we?
The place where you are bathed in clinging fire
and it will last forever,
                        burning, burning,
and you will beg to die.
                    But you can't die
because, poor fool,
                you are already dead.

He'd wipe his forehead with a handkerchief.
If you should die tonight where will your soul
reside for all eternity?
                    In fire?
Or will you sit, in grace, at God's right hand?

GETTING THERE

How far is it?
How far is it now?
The gigantic gorilla interiors
Of the wheels move, they appal me—
The terrible brains
Of Krupp, black muzzles
Revolving, the sound
Punching out Absence! like cannon.
It is Russia I have to get across, it is some war or other.
I am dragging my body
Quietly through the straw of the boxcars.
Now is the time for bribery.
What do wheels eat, these wheels
Fixed to their arcs like gods,
The silver leash of the will—
Inexorable. And their pride!
All the gods know is destinations.
I am a letter in this slot—
I fly to a name, two eyes.
Will there be fire, will there be bread?
Here there is such mud.
It is a trainstop, the nurses
Undergoing the faucet water, its veils, veils in a nunnery,
Touching their wounded,
The men the blood still pumps forward,
Legs, arms piled outside
The tent of unending cries—
A hospital of dolls.
And the men, what is left of the men
Pumped ahead by these pistons, this blood

Into the next mile,
The next hour—
Dynasty of broken arrows!
How far is it?
There is mud on my feet,
Thick, red and slipping. It is Adam's side,
This earth I rise from, and I in agony.
I cannot undo myself, and the train is steaming.
Steaming and breathing, its teeth
Ready to roll, like a devil's.
There is a minute at the end of it
A minute, a dewdrop.
How far is it?
It is so small
The place I am getting to, why are there these obstacles—
The body of this woman,
Charred skirts and deathmask
Mourned by religious figures, by garlanded children.
And now detonations—
Thunder and guns.
The fire's between us.
Is there no still place
Turning and turning in the middle air,
Untouched and untouchable.
The train is dragging itself, it is screaming—
An animal
Insane for the destination,
The bloodspot,
The face at the end of the flare.
I shall bury the wounded like pupas,
I shall count and bury the dead.
Let their souls writhe in a dew,
Incense in my track.
The carriages rock, they are cradles.
And I, stepping from this skin
Of old bandages, boredoms, old faces

Step to you from the black car of Lethe,
Pure as a baby.

THOMAS MCGRATH

THE BLACK TRAIN

I'm still struck (as when I saw my first Pasque-flower)
Now, at a single soft shoot of daffodil arching, slow,
Through the face of the rock-like ground and on: up: through
The flinty shingle of March-blown sleet and snow
On the winter-wasted ice-bound lawns of Milwaukee Avenue.

Spring was a million adjectives: once: one noun:
All green and milky: furry as pussy-willow . . . sweet . . .
As the blood of maple. But the gleamy stealth of gold in the river-
        winding wood
Blurs quicksand or flood. And spider-silk blinds and binds.
Then mullein, purslane, milfoil, milkweed, dandelions . . . tiresome.

Summer wearies me . . . Endless the combers of wheat: gold:
Endless in amber distance. And the endless dance of the aspenleaf
Tires. No new word in the mile-long rasp and rattle: endless
Corn-gossip. The grasshopper burdens and the humblebee is
        no friend.
But I'm glad the homeless sleep warm in this landlords' season.

Autumn tires and conspires: draws forth its druggy water
Where the dreamy souls of strolling poets drown, slow,
In their little ecstasies. Troll fire seams the north woods:
Ghosts of goatsbeard false bird's nests of Queen Anne's lace
Tourists divining with goldenrod beside sluggish rivers . . .

Stern winter frowns. A stiffening mortal rigor
Sets flowerheads rolling and the crowns of summer fall.
Moral as death, a white stealth, cold, beards all the grass
That robes, on sunny thrones in its last and desperate green: false.
False-foxy all: the green of autumn and the gold of spring.

I've lived inland too long. It sickens me—
Land islanded. Winter may harden. But spring unties
All icy strings. Fools'-gold of summer. Treacherous trollopy autumn . . .
No. Enough of this comic death-dance. I long, in mortal longing,
For the shine and silence, the flash and wallop of the sea.

Somewhere in that sea, still, on a tide-bound salt siding,
Hunched, a black train halts, sighing and clanking, slouched,
   and crafty,
Breathing like a rusty pump and waiting for bills of lading.
The telegraph office clicks its beads and abacus, ticks and chatters,
And the empty cars wait for the black train to head inland.

ANONYMOUS

LITTLE BLACK TRAIN IS A-COMIN'

God tole Hezykiah
In a message from on high:
Go set yo' house in ordah,
For thou shalt sholy die.
He turned to the wall an' a-weepin',
Oh! see the King in tears;
He got his bus'ness fixed all right,
God spared him fifteen years.

   Chorus:
   Little black train is a-comin',
   Get all yo' bus'ness right;

Go set yo' house in ordah,
For the train may be here tonight.

Go tell that ball room lady,
All filled with worldly pride,
That little black train is a-comin',
Prepare to take a ride.
That little black train and engine
An' a little baggage car,
With idle thoughts and wicked deeds,
Must stop at the judgment bar.

There was a po' young man in darkness,
Cared not for the gospel light.
Suddenly a whistle blew
From a little black train in sight.
"Oh, death, will you not spare me?
I'm just in my wicked plight.
Have mercy, Lord, do hear me,
Pray come an' set me right."
But death had fixed his shackles
About his soul so tight,
Just befo' he got his bus'ness fixed,
The train rolled in that night.

ADRIENNE RICH

LUCIFER IN THE TRAIN

Riding the black express from heaven to hell
He bit his fingers, watched the countryside,
Vernal and crystalline, forever slide
Beyond his gaze: the long cascades that fell
Ribboned in sunshine from their sparkling height,
The fishers fastened to their pools of green
By silver lines; the birds in sudden flight—
All things the diabolic eye had seen
Since heaven's cockcrow. Imperceptibly
That landscape altered: now in paler air
Tree, hill and rock stood out resigned, severe,
Beside the strangled field, the stream run dry.

Lucifer, we are yours who stiff and mute
Ride out of worlds we shall not see again,
And watch from windows of a smoking train
The ashen prairies of the absolute.
Once out of heaven, to an angel's eye
Where is the bush or cloud without a flaw?
What bird but feeds upon mortality,
Flies to its young with carrion in its claw?
O foundered angel, first and loneliest
To turn this bitter sand beneath your hoe,
Teach us, the newly-landed, what you know;
After our weary transit, find us rest.

LOUISE GLÜCK

DEPARTURE

My father is standing on a railroad platform.
Tears pool in his eyes, as though the face
glimmering in the window were the face of someone
he was once. But the other has forgotten;
as my father watches, he turns away,
drawing the shade over his face,
goes back to his reading.

And already in its deep groove
the train is waiting with its breath of ashes.

DORIANNE LAUX

THE CHILDREN'S TRAIN

As the train approaches the tunnel, the kids
gear up to scream. They pull the darkening
air into their lungs, keep their eyes wide.
The light withdraws in stages, shrinks away

from the floor, the backsides of seats, slips
down the curved ceiling before leaping
like spooked deer through the open windows.
The brave ones squeal into each other's
disappearing faces, poke and pinch their younger
sister's naked knees, but when even the boney
pilings of the tunnel's arched sides
are gone, the ghosts of windows, they quiet,
their breath chilled and caught, as if death's
cupped hand had squeezed their silly mouths shut.
Blind and dumb, deafened by the procession
of slotted wheels ground into metal tracks,
they are hurled through the earth in cars
heavy as caskets. They can feel the borders
of their bodies recede, their curled insides
dissolve, and when they are little more than warm
pits of fear, the lit ribs of the tunnel
return, the bare stone walls that glide past
the windows, offering their small slabs of light.
Their blank faces emerge luminous, filmed
with sweat, emptied, awed by an inkling
that they might not live forever, hands
folded in their laps, a posture curiously
religious as they are pulled
into the frightening brilliance of the world.

GARY SOTO

WHO WILL KNOW US?

For Jaroslav Seifert

It is cold, bitter as a penny.
I'm on a train, rocking toward the cemetery
To visit the dead who now
Breathe through the grass, through me,
Through relatives who will come
And ask, Where are you?
Cold. The train with its cargo
Of icy coal, the conductor
With his loose buttons like heads of crucified saints,
His mad puncher biting zeros through tickets.

The window that looks onto its slate of old snow.
Cows. The barbed fences throat-deep in white.
Farm houses dark, one wagon
With a shivering horse.
This is my country, white with no words,
House of silence, horse that won't budge
To cast a new shadow. Fence posts
That are the people, spotted cows the machinery
That feed Officials. I have nothing
Good to say. I love Paris
And write, "Long Live Paris!"
I love Athens and write,
"The great book is still in her lap."
Bats have intrigued me,
The pink vein in a lilac.
I've longed to open an umbrella
In an English rain, smoke
And not give myself away,
Drink and call a friend across the room,

Stomp my feet at the smallest joke.
But this is my country.
I walk a lot, sleep.
I eat in my room, read in my room,
And make up women in my head—
Nostalgia that's the cigarette lighter from before the war,
Beauty that's tears that flow inward to feed its roots.

The train. Red coal of evil.
We're its passengers, the old and young alike.
Who will know us when we breathe through the grass?

DAVID ST. JOHN

IRIS

Vivian St. John (1891–1974)

There is a train inside this iris:

You think I'm crazy, & like to say boyish
& outrageous things. No, there is

A train inside this iris.

It's a child's finger bearded in black banners.
A single window like a child's nail,

A darkened porthole lit by the white, angular face

Of an old woman, or perhaps the boy beside her in the stuffy,
Hot compartment. Her hair is silver, & sweeps

Back off her forehead, onto her cold & bruised shoulders.

The prairies fail along Chicago. Past the five
Lakes. Into the black woods of her New York; & as I bend

Close above the iris, I see the train

Drive deep into the damp heart of its stem, & the gravel
Of the garden path

Cracks under my feet as I walk this long corridor

Of elms, arched
Like the ceiling of a French railway pier where a boy

With pale curls holding

A fresh iris is waving goodbye to a grandmother, gazing
A long time

Into the flower, as if he were looking some great

Distance, or down an empty garden path & he believes a man
Is walking toward him, working

Dull shears in one hand; & now believe me: The train
Is gone. The old woman is dead, & the boy. The iris curls,
On its stalk, in the shade

Of those elms: Where something like the icy & bitter fragrance

In the wake of a woman who's just swept past you on her way
Home

& you remain.

ROBERT BLY

LOOKING AT NEW-FALLEN SNOW FROM A TRAIN

Snow has covered the next line of tracks,
And filled the empty cupboards in the milkweed pods;
It has stretched out on the branches of weeds,
And softened the frost-hills, and the barbed-wire rolls
Left leaning against a fencepost—
It has drifted onto the window ledges high in the peaks of barns.

    A man throws back his head, gasps
    And dies. His ankles twitch, his hands open and close,
    And the fragment of time that he has eaten is exhaled from his pale
        mouth to nourish the snow.
    A salesman falls, striking his head on the edge of the counter.

Snow has filled out the peaks on the tops of rotted fence posts.
It has walked down to meet the slough water,
And fills all the steps of the ladder leaning against the eaves.
It rests on the doorsills of collapsing children's houses,
And on transformer boxes held from the ground forever in the center
    of cornfields.

    A man lies down to sleep.
    Hawks and crows gather around his bed.
    Grass shoots up between the hawks' toes.
    Each blade of grass is a voice.
    The sword by his side breaks into flame.

DAVID WOJAHN

PHOTO OF MY FATHER IN A SNOWBOUND TRAIN

Now that his name has turned to elegy,
The drifts compose their inexact refrain

As they did in Minnesota every January,
Less a music than a bone white flurry

Of notes calling forth this slide show in my brain,
Where I watch his face turn to elegy,

Then turn away. The snow will drift and bury
Memory and every patch of ground. The Great Northern

Stalled en route to Winnipeg, a January
Blizzard, '61. And here my father stays,

Long pulls from a bourbon flask, alone inside the engine.
The Empire Builder: its very name an elegy

To eras of diesel and steam. No clarity
To the slide: glint of the flask, a drift-bound train,

Gray light of Minnesota January.
Erasure, erasure, visibility

Collapsed to zero. Just an arm now, lifting bourbon
To the disembodied mouth, this elegy

That was his name, blurring to infinity,
Lost in the blizzard's relentless implosions,

Lost to this Minnesota January,
Where his name has turned to snow, to elegy.

RICHARD HUGO

_____

ELEGY

_____

In memory, Harold Herndon

I expected him to look dead in the casket,
you know, waxy, blue tinge, but he looked
dozing and tanned, and I wanted to poke him
in front of the crowd and say, "Harold, time
to get up. No train to drive today. I brought
you a drink. I heard a new joke. Look. Outside, the sun."

I tried to remember his life. He gave
it to me in pieces over the years: parents
dead early, some orphanage in Belgrade,
Montana, or Manhattan, Montana,
how he came to be a train engineer,
how he came to own the dear bar.
I remember the unobtrusive, tentative
way he introduced himself 17 years ago
and how, my life seemingly a wreck, I wanted him
to be there like a boulder beside the river,
put there by experts to lean on,
to sleep in the shade of.
I used him plenty. I paid him back
what I could, mostly a poem, and now and then
drinking our way right into dawn.

He sold the bar when I was in Scotland.
He went on driving the train, the Helena run,
long leisurely freights. My need of him
had run out and I felt better, felt now
when we met I could give something to him.
I need ask nothing, but this morning I feel

like asking someone a hell of a lot
before the freight pulls out, the freight certain
to be tough going and slow, loaded to the limit
by the heaviest star in the firmament.

STERLING A. BROWN

SISTER LOU

Honey
When de man
Calls out de las' train
You're gonna ride,
Tell him howdy.

Gather up yo' basket
An' yo' knittin' an' yo' things,
An' go on up an' visit
Wid frien' Jesus fo' a spell.

Show Marfa
How to make yo' greengrape jellies,
An' give po' Lazarus
A passel of them Golden Biscuits.

Scald some meal
Fo' some rightdown good spoonbread
Fo' li'l box-plunkin' David.

An' sit aroun'
An' tell them Hebrew Chillen
All yo' stories . . .

Honey
Don't be feared of them pearly gates,
Don't go 'round to de back,
No mo' dataway
Not evah no mo'.

Let Michael tote yo' burden
An' yo' pocketbook an' evahthing
'Cept yo' Bible,
While Gabriel blows somp'n
Solemn but loudsome
On dat horn of his'n.

Honey
Go straight on to de Big House,
An' speak to yo' God
Widout no fear an' tremblin'.

Then sit down
An' pass de time of day awhile.

Give a good talkin' to
To yo' favorite 'postle Peter,
An' rub the po' head
Of mixed-up Judas,
An' joke awhile wid Jonah.

Then, when you gits de chance,
Always rememberin' yo' raisin',
Let 'em know youse tired
Jest a mite tired.

Jesus will find yo' bed fo' you
Won't no servant evah bother wid yo' room.
Jesus will lead you

To a room wid windows
Openin’ on cherry trees an’ plum trees
Bloomin’ everlastin’.

An’ dat will be yours
Fo’ keeps.

Den take yo’ time. . . .
Honey, take yo’ bressed time.

DONALD HALL
_____

A SISTER ON THE TRACKS
_____

Between pond and sheepbarn, by maples and watery birches,
Rebecca paces a double line of rust
in a sandy trench, striding on black
creosoted eight-by-eights.
                    In nineteen-forty-three,
wartrains skidded tanks,
airframes, dynamos, searchlights, and troops
to Montreal. She counted cars
from the stopped hayrack at the endless crossing:
ninety-nine, one-hundred . . . and her grandfather Ben’s
voice shaking with rage and oratory told
how the mighty Boston and Maine
kept the Statehouse in its pocket.
                    Today Rebecca walks
a line that vanishes, in solitude

bypassed by wars and commerce. She remembers the story
of the bunting'd day her great-great-great-
grandmother watched the first train roll and smoke
from Potter Place to Gale
with fireworks, cider, and speeches. Then the long rail
drove west, buzzing and humming; the hive of rolling stock
extended a thousand-car'd perspective
from Ohio to Oregon, where men who left stone farms
rode rails toward gold.
                  On this blue day she walks
under a high jet's glint of swooped aluminum pulling
its feathery contrail westward. She sees ahead
how the jet dies into junk, and highway wastes
like railroad. Beside her the old creation retires,
hayrack sunk like a rowboat
under its fields of hay. She closes her eyes
to glimpse the vertical track that rises
from the underworld of graves,
soul's ascension connecting dead to unborn, rails
that hum with a hymn of continual vanishing
where tracks cross.
                For she opens her eyes to read
on a solitary gravestone next to the rails
the familiar names of Ruth and Matthew Bott, born
in a Norfolk parish, who ventured
the immigrant's passionate Exodus westward to labor
on their own land. Here love builds
its mortal house, where today's wind carries
a double scent of heaven and cut hay.

A WALK

I took a walk on the railroad track.
Followed that for a while
and got off at the country graveyard
where a man sleeps between
two wives. Emily van der Zee,
Loving Wife and Mother,
is at John van der Zee's right.
Mary, the second Mrs. van der Zee,
also a Loving Wife, to his left.
First Emily went, then Mary.
After a few years, the old fellow himself.
Eleven children came from these unions.
And they, too, would all have to be dead now.
This is a quiet place. As good a place as any
to break my walk, sit, and provide against
my own death, which comes on.
But I don't understand, and I don't understand.
All I know about this fine, sweaty life,
my own or anyone else's,
is that in a little while I'll rise up
and leave this astonishing place
that gives shelter to dead people. This graveyard.
And go. Walking first on one rail
and then the other.

V. THE EMPIRE WILDERNESS

OF FREIGHT AND RAILS

Three boxcars slept, as quiet as cows.
They were so tired, they'd been so far.
SP and Katy, L & N RR—
After bumble and bang, and where God knows,
They'd cracked the rust of a weed-rank spur, for this pale repose.
—Robert Penn Warren, from "Man in Moonlight"

JOHN FREDERICK NIMS

FREIGHT

. . . the world and all her train . . .
—Henry Vaughn

1

Call Awe, then, what you will, long long ago
It set the heavenly Wheels in locomotion,
Lit stars to warn or beckon, set aflow
The salt of blood, express, from local ocean.
Soon man, with eye aglow and tongue that muttered,
(Banished from Eden's air? or pride of apes?)
Sat clinking flint on flint, and as they shattered
Snatched with a grin what fell in craftier shapes.

The law was move or die. Lively from tigers,
Dainty on deer. Survival called the tune.
Oxen, we learned, would bear us. So would rivers.
And that was science. On the whole a boon.
With hands that worried flint till tools accrue,
We tunneled mountains and rode cozy through.

2

We move, lock, stock, and barrel, all our store.
We *carry*—the word sings with care and courage!
The child, we say, is carried months before
It sees the sky. When grown, we approve its carriage.
True voices carry far; far voices ringing
Carry us back to an old Virginia dream.
The brave say, Carry on. Last, the low-swinging
Sweet chariot coming, for to carry us home.

⟨ 121 ⟩

Life's what we carry, as blood carries air.
Nations have lifeblood: the bright veins of steel
Carry in cars our treasure-trove and care—
Often survival rode the coupled wheel.
Men in the cave flaked stone, were learning how
They'd hew horizons into Here and Now.

3

Clouds are roulette-wheel of the heaven's weather;
The planets wheel, nightlong, in pride of place;
Wheels jewel the wrist, alert us: pain or pleasure;
—And one chilled-iron wheel confounded space.
What caveman on a round rock come a cropper
Rubbed at a rueful hip, brow furrowing *Why?*
Saw granite on loose gravel slip and quiver
Until—a dazzle of wheel-thought like sunrise!

History moved massive on that wheel, until
Boxcars, dark crimson as rich freighted blood,
Streamed from a central heart, made cities tall,
As if the very trains arose and stood
On end, tiered up together, scraping sky.
Pale gondolas of cloud go deadhead by.

4

Set any wheel to earth, and two wheels meet:
Ours and the planet's ponderous wheel of stone
Rough with tectonic rubble, ridge and plate;
Yet both turn easy, like the wheels we've known.
Athens cut ruts of marble: ivory courses
Shunted Apollo's car of solar gold;
John Donne saw wagon-ways; the horse-power, horses.
Over the flats of Kansas sail-cars rolled.

First planks on yielding ground, then treads of metal,
Then steel set edgewise, over stone for ties.

A mountain? Sawtooth rail or crank-and-cable
Till iron took serene the incredulous rise.
Always a tingling rumor in the rail
Kept the one burden humming there: *Prevail*.

5

See the world pitched and tossed. The nerves of matter,
Tougher than cable, hawser hills in place.
Most stubborn stuff, it wills to cling together;
Huddling in love, won't slacken its embrace.
Move it we must though, chipping to our purpose
Irascible flint, blasting the mountain side;
Flexing the tensions our way or they warp us.
Time's a spring too; it tightens when denied.

Railroads, you toy with time, think time your bauble;
You run on time, shrink time, cut time in two.
Do time all kinds of wrong, bind *time* to *table*,
Brag that tomorrow is today for you.
Your goal: arrive—though heat, hail, heaven's fire
Snatch at the brass and varnish of the Flyer.

6

Compleat with a nifty moniker, *Puffing Billy*,
Tom Thumb or *Rocket*, *General*, *Pioneer*,
Cycloped (horse on treadmill sweating), jolly
Sans Pareil, gloss and gold—they, year by year
Flew in the face of time and testy weather,
Enemies both, the lanterned trainmen know.
(By stoves where sand is baking crisp, they gather,
Trading the tall tales of high-striding snow.)

Through juniper in Utah, Pennsy tupelo,
Yucca round Tucson, tamarack in Vermont,
Engines with lamp, stack, bell—caboose with cupola—

Cowcatcher proud as Roman prow, they vaunt
Their way across the continent, huffy vassals
Hooting at towermen in their spidery castles.

7

Best Friend of Charleston, Wabash Cannonball,
Are legend now; but emblems, gold and sable,
Recall them: beaver, mountain goat, the tall
Sequoia or snowy Shasta, robed in fable,
War bonnets of the Salt Lake Road, or torrid
Many-rayed sunset, blazoning their desire
To wrestle the jeweled tiara from Time's forehead,
Set records: *Express* or *Limited, Special, Flyer.*

In Promontory, Utah, '69,
The golden spike uniting East and West
Was sledged in creosote: high iron's sign,
Past roundhouse, shoo-fly shunting, toward their vast
Envisioning. And the spike held, tight as true
Fingers that lock in love and won't undo.

8

The lone prairie, the twilight gray as steel,
The vanishing freight—oh see the lonely road
Our fathers wandered, stumbling on the wheel,
—Daydreamers all, and the long row unhoed—
Sky-hankering men, their reverence still alive
Some years ago: with burning glass and sun
George Stephenson in 1825
Snatched fire for *Locomotion No. 1.*

Ten miles an hour, "immoderate" twelve—so once.
Slow Down to Ninety warns the black ravine.
Smoke-plumed, in armor, as with leveled lance

Engines career, as signals clear to green.
Time brought the caveman, chipper, all this way,
Far from the misty fens of yesterday.

ALLEN GINSBERG
_____

SUNFLOWER SUTRA
_____

I walked on the banks of the tincan banana dock and sat down
    under the huge shade of a Southern Pacific locomotive to
    look at the sunset over the box house hills and cry.
Jack Kerouac sat beside me on a busted rusty iron pole,
    companion, we thought the same thoughts of the soul,
    bleak and blue and sad-eyed, surrounded by the gnarled
    steel roots of trees of machinery.
The oily water on the river mirrored the red sky, sun sank on top
    of final Frisco peaks, no fish in that stream, no hermit in
    those mounts, just ourselves rheumy-eyed and hungover
    like old bums on the riverbank, tired and wily.
Look at the Sunflower, he said, there was a dead gray shadow
    against the sky, big as a man, sitting dry on top of a pile of
    ancient sawdust—
—I rushed up enchanted—it was my first sunflower, memories
    of Blake—my visions—Harlem
and Hells of the Eastern rivers, bridges clanking Joes Greasy
    Sandwiches, dead baby carriages, black treadless tires
    forgotten and unretreaded, the poem of the riverbank,
    condoms & pots, steel knives, nothing stainless, only the

dank muck and the razor sharp artifacts passing into the
     past—
and the gray Sunflower poised against the sunset, crackly bleak
     and dusty with the smut and smog and smoke of olden
     locomotives in its eye—
corolla of bleary spikes pushed down and broken like a battered
     crown, seeds fallen out of its face, soon-to-be-toothless
     mouth of sunny air, sunrays obliterated on its hairy head
     like a dried wire spiderweb,
leaves stuck out like arms out of the stem, gestures from the
     sawdust root, broke pieces of plaster fallen out of the black
     twigs, a dead fly in its ear,
Unholy battered old thing you were, my sunflower O my soul,
     I loved you then!
The grime was no man's grime but death and human locomotives,
all that dress of dust, that veil of darkened railroad skin, that
     smog of cheek, that eyelid of black mis'ry, that sooty hand
     or phallus or protuberance of artificial worse-than-dirt—
     industrial—modern—all that civilization spotting your
     crazy golden crown—
and those blear thoughts of death and dusty loveless eyes and ends
     and withered roots below, in the home-pile of sand and
     sawdust, rubber dollar bills, skin of machinery, the guts and
     innards of the weeping coughing car, the empty lonely
     tincans with their rusty tongues alack, what more could I
     name, the smoked ashes of some cock cigar, the cunts of
     wheelbarrows and the milky breasts of cars, wornout asses
     out of chairs & sphincters of dynamos—all these
entangled in your mummied roots—and you there standing before
     me in the sunset, all your glory in your form!
A perfect beauty of a sunflower! a perfect excellent lovely
     sunflower existence! a sweet natural eye to the new hip
     moon, woke up alive and excited grasping in the sunset
     shadow sunrise golden monthly breeze!
How many flies buzzed round you innocent of your grime, while
     you cursed the heavens of the railroad and your flower soul?
Poor dead flower? when did you forget you were a flower? when
     did you look at your skin and decide you were an impotent
     dirty old locomotive? the ghost of a locomotive? the

〈 126 〉

specter and shade of a once powerful mad American
  locomotive?
You were never no locomotive, Sunflower, you were a sunflower!
And you Locomotive, you are a locomotive, forget me not!
So I grabbed up the skeleton thick sunflower and stuck it at my
  side like a scepter,
and deliver my sermon to my soul, and Jack's soul too, and anyone
  who'll listen,
—We're not our skin of grime, we're not our dread bleak dusty
  imageless locomotive, we're all beautiful golden sunflowers
  inside, we're blessed by our own seed & golden hairy naked
  accomplishment-bodies growing into mad black formal sunflowers in the sunset, spied on by our eyes under the shadow
  of the mad locomotive riverbank sunset Frisco hilly tincan
  evening sitdown vision.

REGINALD GIBBONS

———————————————

AMERICAN TRAINS

———————————————

The Santa Fe, still the one
      that most often sings me its name;
and the rattling Erie & Lackawanna
      that used to ride my first love—
      in whose bed I cried with the thought
      no days would ever be long enough for us—
      to Pennsylvania and school, far
      before I had tried her attention,
      truly, or her forgiveness;

and the always late AMTRAK Montrealer
>that stopped in Massachusetts cornfields
>one night to wait for all the stars
>and American clocks to catch up to it
>as Daylight Savings came on;
and the smoky Conrail commuter
>that rocked and screeched through chemical air
>to New York, a rolling lurching urinal
>carrying bankers and middlemen
>and secretaries smoothing
>their weekday best and putting new lipstick on
>as we coasted out of the tunnel
>into Penn Station and waited—standing
>jammed together with salesmen whose sportcoats
>would never hang right from their tired shoulders,
>and teachers needing new heels, and lawyers—
>waited for the doors to open onto the hot black platform;
and the relic locomotive and open cars
>careening a few miles for tourists in New Jersey,
>the steam engine shocking eyes
>with smoke and coal motes, flushing pheasants
>gaudy with mating out of the trackside brush
>on the back side of shopping centers;
and there's the one you and I got on,
>that started downhill with the weight
>of what we felt and is still in a plummet,
>always and always faster till it has us shaking,
>out of breath, scared . . . "A *freight* train,"
>I said when you asked me, "What *is* this?"

BARRY STERNLIEB

RIGHT OF WAY

What works best
is the mile walk down Sleepy Hollow
to the tracks, fitting weather
into blood until powers merge
     in a single line.
As for this body of land,
it's on the move, but slow as the story
     of how crows
          include the evening,
one of those friends
whose hair is bound
to change, weight up and down,
mind here and there, no more than that.
     Eyeing hello the ruts, heaves,
crumbling shoulder along the creek,
cornfield giving sky a bearded finish,
     yesterday's footprints,
          pines worth being reborn as
over and over until words
never had a chance, finally
stop at the railroad bridge,
     lean downvalley
as tracks bend west
and after awhile that diesel riff
starts to build, full, round, bearlike
through the lowland,
     feel it play the steel
          of the bridge
into arms and legs, louder, triple
locomotives grind a solid clip,

three-minute freight, oilstink, the rock
of boxcars underfoot:
    Boston & Main, a marsh hawk
rides the updraft, gone,
Western Pacific, Delaware & Hudson,
    back home windows rattling now,
        Potlatch, Cotton Belt,
taste the ultimate rust,
flatcars stacked with lumber,
tankcars mapped by grime,
    Santa Fe, Erie Lackawanna,
        Rio Grande the Action Road,
late news banked off veins of sun,
hoppers of gravel, gray on gray,
    Illinois Central Gulf, Southern
Serves the South, height and depth
coupled by motion, creosote wars
in a broken hand,
    Bangor and Aroostook, Soo Line,
a shim of distance,
fills the gap, Norfolk & Western, B & O,
one world after another,
    Union Pacific, Burlington Northern,
in the long run
so much coming and going
it doesn't matter why.

WILLIAM CARLOS WILLIAMS

TO FREIGHT CARS IN THE AIR

all the slow
    clank, clank
    clank, clank
moving above the treetops

the
    wha, wha
of the hoarse whistle

    pah,   pah,   pah
    pah, pah, pah, pah, pah

    piece and piece
    piece and piece
moving still trippingly
through the morningmist

long after the engine
has fought by
            and disappeared

in silence
        to the left

DAVID YOUNG
_____

THE BOXCAR POEM
_____

The boxcars drift by
clanking

they have their own
speech on scored
wood their own
calligraphy
Soo Line
they say in meadows
Lackawanna quick at crossings
Northern Pacific, a
nightmurmur, Northern
Pacific

even empty
they carry
in dark corners
among smells of wood and sacking
the brown wrappings of sorrow
the rank straw of revolution
the persistence of war

and often
as they roll past
like weathered obedient
angels you can see
right through them
to yourself
in a bright
field, a crow
on either shoulder.

ALVIN GREENBERG

FREIGHT TRAIN, FREIGHT TRAIN

all freight, the sudden trains that uncouple my passage home
like flash floods, stranding me in these winter afternoon rains
counting carloads of lumber, flatcars of heavy equipment, sealed
boxcars headed out of the city, cities themselves, miles long
and full of industry, but with only a grim mayor at the throttle
and a handful of sleepy maintenance workers for inhabitants:
where have all the passengers, all the rightful citizens, gone?

in 1940, in the dazed center of my childhood and the last year
before the war—*our* war—we watched my suited, suitcased father
descend the tiled concourse to board "the james whitcomb riley"
at cincinnati's brand-new, brassy, domed and cavernous, art-
decoed union terminal with its floor-to-ceiling mosaics of labor
and industry. almost empty even then, it echoed with the hard
departures of newsstands, shoeshine boys, our own hurried heels
on the marble floors. then it was troop trains, troop trains,
all troop trains: the long, thrilling, khaki freight of the war.

but what did we know of trains then? of industrious engineers
hauling their boxcars of battered freight across the cavernous
wastes of europe to stoke the engines of empire like so much
kindling? of winters thick with the smoke of coal and flesh?
no wonder we take to the air now, or sit in our cars, dreaming,
while the long cities of the dead roll by. somewhere, even then,
there must have been a citizen stopped at a level crossing on a
winter day just like this, motor turned off to save the precious
fuel, counting the rattling box cars, thick with the nostalgia
only these cold rains can bring, ignorant, dreaming of trains.

STANLEY PLUMLY

FOR ESTHER

1

From the back it looks like a porch,
portable, the filigree railing French.

And Truman, Bess and the girl each come out
waving, in short sleeves, because the heat
is worse than Washington.

The day is twelve hours old, Truman is talking.
You tell me to pay attention,

                        so I have my ball-
cap in my hands when he gets to the part that the sun

is suicidal, his dry voice barely audible above the train.

It makes a noise like steam.
He says, he says, he says.

His glasses silver in the sun. He says
there is never enough, and leans down to us.

2

Shultz and I put pennies on the track to make
the train jump. It jumps.

Afternoons you nap—one long pull of the body
through the heat.

⟨ 134 ⟩

I go down to the depot
against orders; it's practically abandoned
except for the guy who hangs out

the mail and looks for pennies. He's president

of this place, he says. We pepper his B & O
brick building with tar balls when he's gone.

You hate the heat and sleep and let
your full voice go when I get caught.

You can't stand my noise or silence.
And I can hear a train in each bent coin.

You're thirty. I still seem to burden that young body.

3

Light bar, dark bar, all the way down. The trick is
if a train comes there is room for only the river.

I look down between the crossties at the Great Miami.
Three miles back, near home,

Kessler has already climbed to his station.
The trick is waiting for the whistle.

                              I remember
your dream about bridges: how, as a child, they shook
you off, something the wind compelled.

You woke up holding on. And now this August morning

I don't know enough to be afraid or care.
I do my thinking here,

looking down at the long ladder on the water,
forty feet below.

〈 135 〉

4

The engine at idle, coasting in the yard, the call bell
back and forth, back and forth above the lull . . .

I hang on like the mail as the cars lock in
to one another, couple, and make a train.

The time I break my arm you swear
me to the ground—no more rivers,
no more side-car rides—

                           and stay up half
the night to rub my legs to sleep.

Sometimes you talk as if Roosevelt

were still alive. Recovery is memory.
I never broke my arm.

               Back and forth. The names
of the states pass every day in front of us, single-file.

5

If a house were straw there'd be a wind,
if a house were wood there'd be a fire,

if a house were brick there'd be a track
and a train to tell the time.

                    I wish each passage
well—wind, fire, time, people on a train.
From here to there, three minutes, whistle-stop.

And a speech each night, the seconds clicking off.

The whole house shakes—or seems to. At intervals,
the ghost smoke fills

⟨ 136 ⟩

all the windows on the close-in side.
It's our weather. It's what we hear all night,
between Troy and anywhere, what you meant

to tell me, out of the body, out of the body travel.

DAVE SMITH
_____

THE ROUNDHOUSE VOICES
_____

In full glare of sunlight I came here, man-tall but thin
as a pinstripe, and stood outside the rusted fence
with its crown of iron thorns while
the soot cut into our lungs with tiny diamonds.
I walked through houses with my grain-lovely slugger
from Louisville that my uncle bought and stood
in the sun that made its glove soft on my hand
until I saw my chance to crawl under and get past
anyone who would demand a badge and a name.

The guard hollered that I could get the hell from there quick
when I popped in his face like a thief. All I ever wanted
to steal was life and you can't get that easy
in the grind of a railyard. *You can't catch me
lardass, I can go left or right good as the Mick,*
I hummed to him, holding my slugger by the neck
for a bunt laid smooth where the coal cars
jerked and let me pass between tracks
until, in a slide on ash, I fell safe and heard
the wheeze of his words: *Who the hell are you, kid?*

I hear them again tonight, Uncle, hard as big brakeshoes,
when I lean over your face in the box of silk. The years
you spent hobbling from room to room alone crawl
up my legs and turn this house to another
house, round and black as defeat, where slugging
comes easy when you whip the gray softball over
the glass diesel globe. Footsteps thump on the stairs
like that fat ball against bricks and when I miss
I hear you warn me to watch the timing, to keep
my eyes on your hand and forget the fence,

hearing also that other voice that keeps me out and away
from you on a day worth playing good ball. Hearing
Who the hell . . . I see myself, like a burning speck
of cinder come down the hill and through a tunnel
of porches like stands, running on deep ash,
and I give him the finger, whose face still gleams
clear as a B & O headlight, just to make him get up
and chase me into a dream of scoring at your feet.
At Christmas that guard staggered home sobbing,
the thing in his chest tight as a torque wrench.
In the summer I did not have to run and now

who is the one who dreams of a drink as he leans over
tools you kept bright as a first-girl's promise? I
have no one to run from or to, nobody to give
my finger to as I steal his peace. Uncle, the light
bleeds on your gray face like the high barbed wire
shadows I had to get through and maybe you don't remember
you said to come back, to wait and you'd show me
the right way to take a hard pitch
in the sun that shudders on the ready man. I'm here

though this is a day I did not want to see. In the roundhouse
the rasp and heel-click of compressors is still,
soot lies deep in every greasy fingerprint.
I called you from the pits and you did not come up
and I felt the fear when I stood on the tracks
that are like stars which never lead us

into any kind of light and I don't know who'll
tell me now when the guard sticks his blind snoot
between us: take off and beat the bastard out.
Can you hear him over the yard, grabbing his chest,
cry out *Who the goddamn hell are you, kid?*

I gave him every name in the book, Uncle, but he caught us
and what good did all those hours of coaching do?
You lie on your back, eyeless forever, and I think
how once I climbed to the top of a diesel and stared
into that gray roundhouse glass where, in anger,
you threw up the ball and made a star
to swear at greater than the Mick ever dreamed.
It has been years but now I know what followed there
every morning the sun came up, not light
but the puffing bad-bellied light of words.

All day I have held your hand, trying to say back that life,
to get under that fence with words I lined
and linked up and steamed into a cold room
where the illusion of hope means skin torn in boxes
of tools. The footsteps come pounding into words
and even the finger I give death is words
that won't let us be what we wanted, each one
chasing and being chased by dreams in a dark place.
Words are all we ever were and they did us
no damn good. Do you hear that?

Do you hear the words that, in oiled gravel, you gave me
when you set my feet in the right stance to swing?
They are coal-hard and they come in wings
and loops like despair not even the Mick
could knock out of this room, words softer
than the centers of hearts in guards or uncles,
words skinned and numbed by too many bricks.
I have had enough of them and bring them back here
where the tick and creak of everything dies
in your tiny starlight and I stand down
on my knees to cry, *Who the hell are you, kid?*

PHILIP LEVINE

AND THE TRAINS GO ON

We stood at the back door
of the shop in the night air
while a line of box cars
of soured wheat and pop bottles
uncoupled and was sent creaking
down our spur. Once, when I
unsealed a car and the two
of us strained the door open
with a groan of rust, an old man
stepped out and tipped his hat.
'It's all yours, boys!'
and he went off, stiff-legged,
smelling of straw and shit.
I often wonder whose father
he was and how long he kept
moving until the police
found him, ticketless, sleeping
in a 2nd class waiting room
and tore the cardboard box
out of his hands and beat him
until the ink of his birth smudged
and surrendered its separate vowels.
In the great railyard of Milano
the dog with the white throat
and the soiled muzzle crossed
and recrossed the tracks
'searching for his master,'
said the boy, but his grandfather
said, 'No. He was sent by God

to test the Italian railroads.'
When I lie down at last to sleep
inside a boxcar of coffins bound
for the villages climbing north
will I waken in a small station
where women have come to claim
what is left of glory? Or will
I sleep until the silver bridge
spanning the Mystic River jabs
me awake, and I am back
in a dirty work-shirt that says *Phil*,
24 years old, hungry and lost, on
the run from a war no one can win?
I want to travel one more time
with the wind whipping in
the open door, with you to keep
me company, back the long
tangled road that leads us home.
Through Flat Rock going east
picking up speed, the damp fields
asleep in moonlight. You stand
beside me, breathing the cold
in silence. When you grip
my arm hard and lean way out
and shout out the holy names
of the lost neither of us is scared
and our tears mean nothing.

MICHAEL COLLIER

NORTH CORRIDOR

Living along the path
of these inconstant tracks
(a spur for shuttling coal),

we've learned to anticipate
the freight that pounds
at night and shakes our home

and stays in us as a dream
of something heavy stays,
foreboding and proximate

but always passing through.
So when a single boxcar
strayed one morning, chalk-

scrawled with siding codes,
creaking and sighing,
but also jingling like coins

in a collection box, we left
our house to stare at it.
And where it came to rest,

a prisoner of the crossing gates,
it stayed until the afternoon—
unclaimed, inscrutable,

locked with metal sealing tape.
Cars shunted around it,
over the rails. Children scaled

its laddered sides and hung
from its chain-locked wheel brake
and fit their necks inside

the couplings' claw-shaped
handcuffs. They did it
for a thrill, for fun,

though no one laughed. Then
in the afternoon two railway men
appeared in their blue truck

and carried long pole pry-jacks
to the wheels and slipped
the iron tongues along the rails

until with only their bodies
they fulcrummed the boxcar
to move just off the crossing,

where it stayed until that night.
When we heard the thrashing, the screech
of metal stretching from the dark

tree-thick right-of-way, it was as if
the mother of us all had come
to claim us, angry, staring us down

with her bright headlight, then butting
our heads, staggering the whole house
behind the engine's sudden lurch.

DENISE LEVERTOV

DON'T YOU HEAR THAT WHISTLE BLOWIN' . . .

The 4 a.m. freight comes pounding and shaking through the fall night
and I go to the Middle Door to watch, through the plain glass that has
    stained glass around it,
pressing my forehead against the pane,

and Steve hurries along to look too—for he's out of Appalachia,
the lonesome romance of the rails West is in his bones;

and Richard comes close behind, gazing intently over my shoulder—
out of the Midwest and the rails West are in his blood,
and our friend Bo is at this very moment hopping freight in Oregon to
    pick pears;

and I seem to smell iron and rust, an animal smell, red and dusty,
even through the glass that's steaming up with our breaths.
So I start to open the door, to hear the last cars and the caboose
    louder
and the sound of going away, and to see the stars,

and I want you, Mitch, to step out with me into the dark garden,
for you're standing back of me too, taller than anyone;

but as the cold air comes in I turn toward you and you're not there.
Then I realize I'm waking up: the train really is going by
but the Middle Door's back in my childhood, not in America,

and there's no one in the house but you and me,
you asleep beside me in bed, and soon you'll have left

and this moment of dark boxcars just visible
under the paling stars, a train of looming forms from faraway states
lurching through the edge of Boston,

is just the beginning of a long train of times I'll turn
to share a vision with you and find I'm dreaming.

JAY PARINI

_____

COAL TRAIN

_____

Three times a night it woke you
in middle summer, the Erie Lackawanna,
running to the north on thin, loud rails.
You could feel it coming a long way off:
at first, a tremble in your belly,
a wire trilling in your veins, then diesel
rising to a froth beneath your skin.
You could see the cowcatcher,
wide as a mouth and eating ties,
the headlight blowing a dust of flies.
There was no way to stop it.
You lay there, fastened to the tracks
and waiting, breathing like a bull,
your fingers lit at the tips like matches.
You waited for the thunder of wheel and bone,
the axles sparking, fire in your spine.
Each passing was a kind of death,
the whistle dwindling to a ghost in air,

the engine losing itself in trees.
In a while, your heart was the loudest thing,
your bed was a pool of night.

GALWAY KINNELL

————————————

LACKAWANNA

————————————

Possibly a child is not damaged immediately
but only after some time has passed.
When the parent who sits on the edge
of the bed leans over and moves an elbow
or a forearm or a hand across the place
where the child's torso divides into legs
at last gets up and goes to the door and turns
and says in an ordinary voice, "Good night,"
then in exactly eight minutes a train
in the freight yards on the other side of town
howls, its boxcar loaded up, its doors
rusted shut, its wheels clacking
over the tracks   *lacka   wanna   lacka.*
It may be that the past has the absolute force
of the law that visits parent upon child
unto the third or fourth generation, and the implacability
of vectors, which fix the way a thing
goes reeling according to where it was touched.
What is called spirit may be the exhaust-light
of toil of the kind a person goes through
years later to take any unretractable step

out of that room, even a step no longer
than a platinum-iridium bar in a vault in Paris,
and flesh the need afterwards to find
the nearest brasserie and mark with both elbows
on the zinc bar the start and the finish.
Never mind. The universe is expanding.
Soon they won't know where to look to find you.
There will be even more room when the sun dies.
It will be eight minutes before we know it is dead.
Plenty of time for the ordinary human acts
that will constitute our final mayhem.
In the case of a house there may be less room
when the principal occupants die, especially
if they refuse to leave and keep on growing.
Then in a few years the immaterial bulk
of one of them padding up from the dark
basement can make the stairs shriek
and the sleeper sit up, pivot out of bed, knock
an arm on the dresser, stand there shaking
while the little bones inside the elbow cackle.
The mind can start rippling again at any time
if what was thrown in was large, and thrown in early.
When the frequency of waves increases,
so does the energy. If pressure builds up,
someone could die from it. If they had been
able to talk with him, find out what he was going through,
the children think it would not have been him.
Inquiring into the situation of a thing
may alter the comportment, size, or shape of it.
The female nurse's elbow, for instance,
bumping a penis, could raise it up,
or the male doctor's hand, picking it up
and letting it drop a couple of times for
unexplained medical reasons, could slacken it.
Or vice versa. And the arm passing across it,
like Ockham's razor grabbed off God's chin
eight minutes before the train howls,
could simplify it nearly out of existence.
Is it possible, even, that Werner Heisenberg,

boy genius, hit on his idea in eight minutes?
The train sounds its horn and clickets over
the tracks   *lacka*   *wanna*   shaking up
a lot of bones trying to lie unnoticed
in the cemeteries. It stops to let off
passengers in a town, as the overturned grail
of copper and tin, lathed and fettled off
to secure its pure minor tierce, booms out
from the sanctus-turret those bulging notes
which, having been heard in childhood,
seem to this day to come from heaven.
So in memory, an elbow, which is without flesh,
touching a penis, which is without bone,
can restart the shock waves of being the one chosen,
even in shame, in a childhood of being left out.
But no one gets off. And a hand
apports in the center of a room suddenly
become empty, which the child has to fill
with something, with anything, with the ether
the Newtonian physicists manufactured
to make good the vacuums in the universe
or the nothing the God of the beginning
suctioned up off the uninhabited earth
and held all this time and now must exhale
back down, making it hard, for some, to breathe.
The hand suspended in the room still has
a look of divinity; every so often
it makes sweet sounds—music can't help it; like maggots
it springs up anywhere. The umbilical string
rubs across the brain, making it
do what it can, sing.

SHERWOOD ANDERSON

EVENING SONG

Back of Chicago the open fields—were you ever there?
Trains coming toward you out of the West—
Streaks of light on the long grey plains?—many a song—
Aching to sing.

I've got a grey and ragged brother in my breast—
That's a fact.

Back of Chicago the open fields—were you ever there?
Trains coming from you into the West—
Clouds of dust on the long grey plains.
Long trains go West, too—in the silence
Always a song—
Waiting to sing.

FREIGHT CARS

Once, taking a train into Chicago
from the west, I saw a message
scrawled on a wall in the railway yard—
Tommy, call home, we need you—
and for years I have worried, imagining
the worst scenarios. Beneath the message
was a number written in red chalk,
although at eighteen who was I to call
and at forty-five who is left to listen?
But Tommy, I think of him still traveling
out in the country, riding freight car
after freight car, just squeaking by
in pursuit of some private quest.
That's the problem, isn't it?
Coming into this world and imagining
some destination for oneself,
some place to make all the rest
all right, as we cast aside those
who love us, as they cast aside others
in their turn, and all of us
wandering, wandering in a direction
which only our vanity claims to be forward,
while the messages fall away like pathetic cries—
come back, call home, we need you.

CONRAD HILBERRY

BODY AND MIND

Body and mind, we used to think, were two
freight trains, travelling side by side,
the stunt man making the incredible leap
from one to the other. They now appear to be
one train, or rather one long animal
growing across Iowa, inventing
itself as it goes. Mile after mile
it comes into its own, rushing forward
from what it was, taking into itself
the cows and silos, the farmers in pickup trucks,
the slopes and gullies of the landscape.

Body is the created animal—
the ribs and scales that have actually
occurred, everything that time has settled.
Mind works at the edge where a new creature
twists out of its past; mind lures it west
beyond the finished fact which is Dubuque.

JAMES WRIGHT

OUTSIDE FARGO, NORTH DAKOTA

Along the sprawled body of the derailed Great Northern freight car,
I strike a match slowly and lift it slowly.
No wind.

Beyond town, three heavy white horses
Wade all the way to their shoulders
In a silo shadow.

Suddenly the freight car lurches.
The door slams back, a man with a flashlight
Calls me good evening.
I nod as I write good evening, lonely
And sick for home.

DAVE ETTER

GREAT NORTHERN

1

What is it about a Great Northern boxcar,
standing on a cold siding in Minneapolis,
that fills me with such nameless joy?

2

Wave, boy, that's *The Winnipeg Limited*!

3

Inarticulate, lacking paper words,
I celebrate the railroads in my blood.

4

Have you ever ridden *The Western Star*?

5

Through the snowfields of central Minnesota
The Empire Builder plunges into the night,
and I shake by the thundering tracks,
crying hoarsely: "Love, love, love."

6

Trains, the beautiful, goddamn trains.

⟨ 153 ⟩

DAVID WOJAHN

RIDING THE EMPIRE BUILDER, 1948

My father in the snowy window, face incandescent
And the sky all day going on with its labors
Like a man throwing mailsacks from a train, long descent
From Whitefish to the plains, and in the corner
Of his eye he can only see steam, engine straining
Away from Badlands to the Minnesota border,
And it snows all the way from Fergus Falls, staining
The landscape to bone, until the scene is ordered
Around the orange glow of his Camel, the stove
And its butane purr, and the last hundred miles
He dozes on a mailsack, chamois work gloves,
The Browning automatic on the table, aisle upon aisle
Of mail, and here a stranger's coffin bound express
For where he's going too, crossed hands drowsing on his chest.

MICHAEL PETTIT

SELF-PORTRAIT APPROACHING PROMONTORY, UTAH

Again today it is
disciplined thought I'm after,
clear as the blue mountain
air into which a white boa of smoke
rises. Below, naturally,
is the locomotive and I think
about trains of thought, how long
they are, coal car after coal car
after coal car pulling up the grade.
Think about the rails and ties,
about the rock roadbed
and the grease on the rocks
and the stubs of flares
and the conductor in the caboose
with its pot-bellied stove,
and the pot-bellied engineer
with his head out the window,
spitting tobacco, his hand resting
on the wide-open throttle.
And think what would happen
if slowly and for no reason
he knows, the conductor starts
to uncouple the cars, caboose first,
then coal car after coal car
after coal car. The leaping conductor
bidding each in turn good-bye,
unattached and in perfect order
they'd go rolling back down
the mountain so that the smoke
from the smokestack blows

horizontal as the scenery
slowly goes by faster and faster
until the engineer finally notices
and spits and thinks Shit
now what could be happening now?

PHILIP BOOTH
─────────────

CROSSING
─────────

STOP   LOOK   LISTEN
as gate stripes swing down,
count the cars hauling distance
upgrade through town:
warning whistle, bellclang,
engine eating steam,
engineer waving,
a fast-freight dream:
B&M boxcar,
boxcar again,
Frisco gondola,
eight-nine-ten,
Erie and Wabash,
Seaboard, U.P.,
Pennsy tankcar,
twenty-two, three,
Phoebe Snow, B&O,
thirty-four, five,

Santa Fe cattle
shipped alive,
red cars, yellow cars,
orange cars, black,
Youngstown steel
down to Mobile
on Rock Island track,
fifty-nine, *sixty*,
hoppers of coke,
Anaconda copper,
hotbox smoke,
eighty-eight,
red-ball freight,
Rio Grande,
Nickel Plate,
Hiawatha,
Lackawanna,
rolling fast
and loose,
ninety-seven,
coal car,
boxcar,
CABOOSE!

JAMES TATE

MANNA

I do remember some things
times when I listened and heard
no one saying no, certain
miraculous provisions
of the much prayed for manna
and once a man, it was two
o'clock in the morning in
Pittsburg, Kansas, I finally
coming home from the loveliest
drunk of them all, a train chugged,
goddamn, struggled across a
prairie intersection and
a man from the caboose really waved, honestly, and said,
and said something like my name.

LAURA JENSEN

TO A STRANGER (AT THE END OF A CABOOSE)

There is a sway that comes soon after
a question. Oatheart, riding a train
in another language, turns from tense
to tense around a verb wheel, its maze
and answer like an angel that missed Adam
and followed like a leaf into traffic.

Summer was a boxcar, never abandoned,
never reclaimed. Summer was unsteady
in detail. He had coveted the thistles
from Rock Island to the Reading,
and seen from a train vitality;
there's more to a farm than patience.

But here are the children side by side
apart from the arty barren farmhouse, really
traveling with the weight of the stack
of their pumpkins, each hauled from the vine
like a suitcase or a sack of money.

In the inner wheel of Oatheart's head
they are traveling farther than the road
from the world in their winter backdrop;
traveling themselves, why not? Changed
by the train wheel, and by afterthoughts.

DAVID YOUNG

A PROJECT FOR FREIGHT TRAINS

Sitting at crossings and waiting for freights to pass, we have all noticed words—COTTON BELT / ERIE / BE SPECIFIC—SAY UNION PACIFIC / SOUTHERN SERVES THE SOUTH—going by. I propose to capitalize on this fact in the following way:

All freight cars that have high solid sides—boxcars, refrigerator cars, tank cars, hopper cars, cement cars—should be painted one of eight attractive colors, and have one large word printed on them:

1. Burnt orange freight cars with the word CLOUD in olive drab.
2. Peagreen freight cars with the word STAR in charcoal gray.
3. Rose-red freight cars with the word MEADOW in salmon pink.
4. Glossy black freight cars with the word STEAM in gold.
5. Peach-colored freight cars with the word AIR in royal blue.
6. Peach-colored freight cars with the word PORT in forest green.
7. Lavender freight cars with the word GRASS in vermilion or scarlet.
8. Swiss blue freight cars with the word RISING in chocolate brown.

When this has been accomplished, freight cars should continue to be used in the usual ways, so that the word and color combinations will be entirely random, and unpredictable poems will roll across the landscape.

Freight cars without words (i.e., without high or solid sides, such as flatcars, cattle cars, gondolas, automobile transporters, etc.) should all be painted white, to emphasize their function as spaces in the poems. Cabooses can be this color too, with a large black dot, the only punctuation.

Approximations of these random train poems can be arrived at by using the numbers above, plus 9 and 0 for spaces, and combining serial numbers from dollar bills, social security numbers, birthdates, and telephone numbers. The 5-6 combination, which makes AIRPORT, is to be considered a lucky omen. 2-6 may be even luckier.

This project would need to be carried out over the entire United States at once. Every five years a competition could be held among poets to see who can provide the best set of colors and words for the next time.

VI. COACH TRAINS ACROSS

THE SEAMLESS LAND

Journeys are ways of marking out a distance,
Or dealing with the past, however ineffectually,
Or ways of searching for some new enclosure in this space
Between the oceans . . .
—Weldon Kees, from "Travels in North America"

When the train starts, and the passengers are settled
To fruit, periodicals and business letters
(And those who saw them off have left the platform)
Their faces relax from grief to relief,
To the sleepy rhythm of a hundred hours.
Fare forward, travellers! not escaping from the past
Into different lives, or into any future;
You are not the same people who left that station
Or who will arrive at any terminus,
While the narrowing rails slide together behind you . . .
—T. S. Eliot, from "The Dry Salvages"

LANGSTON HUGHES

PENNSYLVANIA STATION

The Pennsylvania Station in New York
Is like some vast basilica of old
That towers above the terrors of the dark
As bulwark and protection to the soul.
Now people who are hurrying alone
And those who come in crowds from far away
Pass through this great concourse of steel and stone
To trains, or else from trains out into day.
And as in great basilicas of old
The search was ever for a dream of God,
So here the search is still within each soul
Some seed to find that sprouts a holy tree
To glorify the earth—and you—and me.

WILLIAM CARLOS WILLIAMS

OVERTURE TO A DANCE OF LOCOMOTIVES

Men with picked voices chant the names
of cities in a huge gallery: promises
that pull through descending stairways
to a deep rumbling.

               The rubbing feet
of those coming to be carried quicken a
grey pavement into soft light that rocks
to and fro, under the domed ceiling,
across and across from pale
earthcoloured walls of bare limestone.

Covertly the hands of a great clock
go round and round! Were they to
move quickly and at once the whole
secret would be out and the shuffling
of all ants be done forever.

A leaning pyramid of sunlight, narrowing
out at a high window, moves by the clock:
disaccordant hands straining out from
a center: inevitable postures infinitely
repeated—
two—twofour—twoeight!
Porters in red hats run on narrow platforms.
This way ma'am!
               —important not to take
the wrong train!
               Lights from the concrete
ceiling hang crooked but—

Poised horizontal
on glittering parallels the dingy cylinders
packed with a warm glow—inviting entry—
pull against the hour. But brakes can
hold a fixed posture till—
                    The whistle!

Not twoeight. Not twofour. Two!

Gliding windows. Colored cooks sweating
in a small kitchen. Taillights—

In time: twofour!
In time: twoeight!

—rivers are tunneled: trestles
cross oozy swampland: wheels repeating
the same gesture remain relatively
stationary: rails forever parallel
return on themselves infinitely.
                    The dance is sure.

RANDALL JARRELL

_____

ON THE RAILWAY PLATFORM

_____

The rewarded porters opening their smiles,
Grapes with a card, and the climate changing
From the sun of bathers to the ice of skis
Cannot hide it—journeys are journeys.

And, arrived or leaving, "Where am I going?"
All the travellers have wept; "is it once again only
The country I laughed at and nobody else?
The passage of a cell between two cells?"

No, the ends are hardly indifferent, the shadow
Falls from our beaches to the shivering floes,
The faces fail while we watch, and darkness
Sucks from the traveller his crazy kiss.

The tears are forming; and the leaver falls
Down tracks no wheel retraces, by the signs
Whose names name nothing, mean: Turn where you may,
You travel by the world's one way.

And the tears fall. What we leave we leave forever:
Time has no travellers. And journeys end in
No destinations we meant. And the strangers
Of all the future turn their helpless gaze

Past the travellers who cannot understand
That they have come back to tomorrow's city,
And wander all night through the unbuilt houses
And take from strangers their unmeant kisses.

MAY SWENSON

RIDING THE "A"

I ride
the "A" train
and feel
like a ball-
bearing in a roller skate.
I have on a gray
rain-
coat. The hollow
of the car
is gray.
My face
a negative in the slate
window,
I sit
in a lit
corridor that races
through a dark
one. Strok-
ing steel,
what a smooth rasp—it feels
like the newest of knives
slicing
along
a long
black crusty loaf
from West 4th to 168th.
Wheels
and rails
in their prime
collide,

make love in a glide
of slickness
and friction.
It is an elation
I wish to pro-
long.
The station
is reached
too soon.

LISEL MUELLER
_____

COMMUTER
_____

How many times have I traveled
into the city
on this train,
always facing
the immediate future,
everything flowing toward me
and, passing, put behind me,
forgettable

Today the conductor
has failed to reverse the seats,
or someone coupled the cars
the wrong way around:
I watch the shabby houses,
the industrial plants, recede

⟨ 170 ⟩

as if they were friends who had seen me off
and were getting smaller and smaller

The heads of the factory vents
bend as if in meditation
as they move out of my sight

I say goodbye to electrical wires
strung like an empty musical score,
to a bright blue knot of pipes,
a blown-up model
of some nexus under my skin,
goodbye to hooded red eyes
that blink at the crossings
with their laconic bells

Even the dirty river
trapped in this city for good
becomes ephemeral
and precious, as I am dragged
across its sun-glazed surface
into the dark station.

KATE DANIELS

THE WOMEN'S ROOM IN PENNSYLVANIA STATION

Covered with rags and cardboard and nothing,
women are lying on the filthy floor.
There is no shame, no disgust here
in their domain where men can't come.

They are squatting nonchalantly on crusted feet
and rinsing tattered nylons
in the public sinks. Their broken bags
are full of broken things busted far
beyond the claims of usefulness or beauty.

For once, in a female place,
there are no tales of pregnancies
or monthlies, or frustrated husbands
playing cruel gods again.
All that must be far behind,
remembered in suburban rooms somewhere,
gold-framed photographs insisting
on histories these women have forgotten

—or forgone in favor
of this transient life enacted
on the cold linoleum of the station john.

Above their heads, the city's cadres
of businessmen rush to work
unmindful of the women two floors below
who keep no homes, raise no tots,
who have no consciousness of what they might
have lost: a man's protection, the sanitary
comfort his wallet brings, a haven
from which they will not be routed,
driven out into streets and weather.

For now, a secretary's lost lipstick
in a gold gilt case, an unbruised apple
for a hasty lunch—these are enough.
Crouched together on the bathroom floor,
the women share a wave of sweet relief
each time the ceiling rumbles
when a train pulls out,
carrying away its cargo of men.

CORNELIA VEENENDAAL

ON MY FOURTEENTH WEDDING

ANNIVERSARY I RIDE ON TRAINS

1

The one-coach Penn Central is bound
for Albany, but it stops at Back Bay
to take on a few commuters.
The conductor gives us a hand
up the back steps and we file in
through the snack bar.
If ever it turns spring
and we have a hot afternoon,
I'll get a can of gingerale.

But today is still as drab
as an Army-Navy store and I
settle down among newspapers
beside the rank ivory wall
and heavy lidded window, under
the tossed coats and shopping bags
on the luggage rack and thank God
for the smooth old pacesetter.
Alongside the turnpike streaks by,
then come the trees and towers
and houses among trees, all
powdered with predicted snow.

Where's my book?

2

The great Pullman was whirling onward
with such dignity of motion . . . the
plains of Texas pouring eastward.

"Ever been in a parlour-car before?"

"No," she answered; "I never was.
It's fine, ain't it?"

"Great! And after a while we'll
go forward to the diner and get
a big lay-out. Finest meal in the world.
Charge a dollar."

"O, do they?" cried the bride.
"Charge a dollar? Why that's too much—
for us—ain't it, Jack?"
"Not this trip," he answered bravely.
"We're going to go the whole thing."

He pointed out the dazzling fittings
and her eyes grew wide as she took in
the sea-green figured velvet,
shining brass, silver and glass,
the wood that gleamed as darkly
brilliant as a pool of oil.
The ceiling was frescoed
in olive and silver. . . .*

*Stephen Crane, The Bride Comes to Yellow Sky.

MAY SWENSON

WRITTEN WHILE RIDING THE

LONG ISLAND RAIL ROAD

Hard water and square wheels.
A foot wears a hat and walks on its thumbs.
        The clouds are of plaster. That hiss is a box.
Honey is hairy. This cipher's a house.
        In a coffin of chocolate the hatchet is laid.
A cactus is sneezing. A blind violin
        has digested a penny. The telephone's juice
has stiffened a horsefly, whose porcelain curse
        is rocking the corridor. Pockets are born,
but the stubble of rainbows cannot be controlled.
        The bite of the barber begins to compete
with the weight of a capsized spondee or stilt.
        The chime of the calendar suffers from rust,
and cobalt is scorched beyond closure or froth.
        If a portion of pinch is applied to a cube,
and scissorlike bubbles produced with a switch,
        we can burnish the windows with faucets and lips.
Will oral implosions enrapture the fish
        so that their lecterns, transparently diced,
while diploid, will dapple? We tried it, and found
        that a petrified lace leaked out of the pistol
of Charlotte, the Kink, while Pug, drunk on lightning,
        slept in the bank with ankles and rabbits
he'd slaughtered with borscht. Snafu just sucked
        on his pommel and barfed. Then let the moon's
carpet display a cartoon: The lawn's perpendicular,

Daddy comes home, and the doorknob's a funnel.
And owl's in the sink. There's a flag in the oven.
    The front page is blank.

DANA GIOIA
_____

IN CHEEVER COUNTRY
_____

Half an hour north of Grand Central
the country opens up. Through the rattling
grime-streaked windows of the coach, streams appear,
pine trees gather into woods, and the leaf-swept yards
grow large enough to seem picturesque.

Farther off smooth parkways curve along the rivers,
trimmed by well-kept trees, and the County Airport
now boasts seven lines, but to know this country
see it from a train—even this crowded local
jogging home half an hour before dark

smelling of smoke and rain-damp shoes
on an afternoon of dodging sun and showers.
One trip without a book or paper
will show enough to understand
this landscape no one takes too seriously.

The architecture of each station still preserves
its fantasy beside the sordid tracks—
defiant pergolas, a shuttered summer lodge,
a shadowy pavilion framed by high-arched windows
in this land of northern sun and lingering winter.

The town names stenciled on the platform signs—
Clear Haven, Bullet Park, and Shady Hill—
show that developers at least believe in poetry
if only as a talisman against the commonplace.
There always seems so much to guard against.

The sunset broadens for a moment, and the passengers
standing on the platform turn strangely luminous
in the light streaming from the palisades across the river.
Some board the train. Others greet their arrivals
shaking hands and embracing in the dusk.

If there is an afterlife, let it be a small town
gentle as this spot at just this instant.
But the car doors close, and the bright crowd,
unaware of its election, disperses to the small
pleasures of the evening. The platform falls behind.

The train gathers speed. Stations are farther apart.
Marble staircases climb the hills where derelict estates
glimmer in the river-brightened dusk.
Some are convents now, some orphanages,
these palaces the Robber Barons gave to God.

And some are merely left to rot where now
broken stone lions guard a roofless colonnade,
a half-collapsed gazebo bursts with tires,
and each detail warns it is not so difficult
to make a fortune as to pass it on.

But splendor in ruins is splendor still,
even glimpsed from a passing train,
and it is wonderful to imagine standing
in the balustraded gardens above the river
where barges still ply their distant commerce.

Somewhere upstate huge factories melt ore,
mills weave fabric on enormous looms,
and sweeping combines glean the cash-green fields.
Fortunes are made. Careers advance like armies.
But here so little happens that is obvious.

Here in the odd light of a rainy afternoon
a ledger is balanced and put away,
a houseguest knots his tie beside a bed,
and a hermit thrush sings in the unsold lot
next to the tracks the train comes hurtling down.

Finally it's dark outside. Through the freight houses
and oil tanks the train begins to slow
approaching the stations where rows of travel posters
and empty benches wait along the platform.
Outside a few cars idle in the sudden shower.

And this at last is home, this ordinary town
where the lights on the hill gleaming in the rain
are the lights that children bathe by, and it is time
to go home now—to drinks, to love, to supper,
to the modest places which contain our lives.

BRENDAN GALVIN

THE OLD TRIP BY DREAM TRAIN

Engine and tender, old loaf-shaped Pullman.
I am making the trip alone
because of the house a dream within this dream
keeps erecting in my sleep.

It is always barely April, but at loading docks
behind the church-topped mills, in the cinders
and shattered weeds, it is late November.

No one is on the streets, no one's not working,
and the workday flashing past looks empty,
the storefronts blind. Not one pane of forty-eight
in a factory window winks; just row on row,
banked like the pigeonholes
in a postal clerk's nightmare.

In a side yard a hairless, vested man
rakes among shadows eloquent as the clang
of steel doors. There are joined angles of bridges,
tanks with coolie hats, a distant refinery
like stacked poker chips,

but always that house, white in April sunlight,
nearly perfect except for broken slats
in the green, nailed shutters.

Then the piney backs of towns, and blond fields
where rocks seem to crawl out of their shadows,
and the slow progressions into small, identical
cities of brown bungalows and triple-deckers,
clatter of Redcaps' dollies, arrival and departure

through which I see the shadow of a crow
crossing white shingles in light so clear
it could be bottled and sold.

Switchyards and sidings, men working gears
with levers, municipal power blocks, trestles,
at one stop the illusion of slipping back
when the cars alongside begin to move;

finally the coast, where a tug trundles upriver
and one seabird crosses high and slow,
a hint of prehistory in its flight,

then cranberry bogs, ditch-ruled and crossed
with levees supporting pump houses,
a set of iron wheels stunned in sunlight.

I try to see the roof of that white place,
the red brick chimney's shadow,
the rainstreak of mortar like a second shadow.

Under cirrus brushwork the creeks
crawl into harbors, their soft tides
feeling seaward in various blues, opening out
under sky opening out.

Crossings too small for gates and lanterns blur by,
each with its warning X,
and one by one, joined by railside wires,
minor stations appear on the line,

a country of white houses whose one-story
bedrooms and late ells meet their barns,
whose oil drums sit on sawhorses.

I stop this trip by its pullcord, and step down
to a sooty cream station trimmed in maroon,
a coalbox alongside, and walk up a two-lane road
nothing is moving on.

The light is always April, chilled amber,
the air headier than I imagined.
Beyond the Big Dipper Dancehall, torn
to its baseposts thirty years ago,

I turn onto a sand road, pass cabins shut
till June, and Ed Mather's place;
he elected to live up hollow from everything
but a deer run and weather.

If I find that house where locust trees
shadow the flaking paint,
will I pry its green storm door and break
the frosted pane over the inside knob,

and enter rooms abandoned to mothballs and
mousedirt and that gray matter that springs out
on old shoes, and call that warehouse
of sheeted furniture home?

HART CRANE

from THE BRIDGE

THE RIVER

. . . and past
the din and
slogans of
the year—

Stick your patent name on a signboard
brother—all over—going west—young man
Tintex—Japalac—Certain-teed Overalls ads
and lands sakes! under the new playbill ripped
in the guaranteed corner—see Bert Williams what?
Minstrels when you steal a chicken just
save me the wing for if it isn't
Erie it ain't for miles around a
Mazda—and the telegraphic night coming on Thomas

a Ediford—and whistling down the tracks
a headlight rushing with the sound—can you
imagine—while an EXPRESS makes time like
SCIENCE—COMMERCE and the HOLYGHOST
RADIO ROARS IN EVERY HOME WE HAVE THE NORTHPOLE
WALLSTREET AND VIRGINBIRTH WITHOUT STONES OR
WIRES OR EVEN RUNning brooks connecting ears
and no more sermons windows flashing roar
breathtaking—as you like it . . . eh?

So the 20th Century—so
whizzed the Limited—roared by and left
three men, still hungry on the tracks, ploddingly
watching the tail lights wizen and converge, slipping gimleted and neatly out of sight.
*
The last bear, shot drinking in the Dakotas
Loped under wires that span the mountain stream.

⟨ 181 ⟩

Keen instruments, strung to a vast precision
Bind town to town and dream to ticking dream. *to those*
But some men take their liquor slow—and count *whose addresses*
—Though they'll confess no rosary nor clue— *are never near*
The river's minute by the far brook's year.
Under a world of whistles, wires and steam
Caboose-like they go ruminating through
Ohio, Indiana—blind baggage—
To Cheyenne tagging . . . Maybe Kalamazoo.

Time's rendings, time's blendings they construe
As final reckonings of fire and snow;
Strange bird-wit, like the elemental gist
Of unwalled winds they offer, singing low
My Old Kentucky Home and *Casey Jones*,
Some Sunny Day. I heard a road-gang chanting so.
And afterwards, who had a colt's eyes—one said,
"Jesus! Oh I remember watermelon days!" And sped
High in a cloud of merriment, recalled
"—And when my Aunt Sally Simpson smiled," he drawled—
"It was almost Louisiana, long ago."
"There's no place like Booneville though, Buddy,"
One said, excising a last burr from his vest,
"—For early trouting." Then peering in the can,
"—But I kept on the tracks." Possessed, resigned,
He trod the fire down pensively and grinned,
Spreading dry shingles of a beard. . . .

                    Behind
My father's cannery works I used to see
Rail-squatters ranged in nomad raillery,
The ancient men—wifeless or runaway
Hobo-trekkers that forever search
An empire wilderness of freight and rails.
Each seemed a child, like me, on a loose perch,
Holding to childhood like some termless play.
John, Jake or Charley, hopping the slow freight
—Memphis to Tallahassee—riding the rods,
Blind fists of nothing, humpty-dumpty clods.

Yet they touch something like a key perhaps.
From pole to pole across the hills, the states
but who have —They know a body under the wide rain;
touched her, Youngsters with eyes like fjords, old reprobates
knowing her With racetrack jargon,—dotting immensity
without name They lurk across her, knowing her yonder breast
Snow-silvered, sumac-stained or smoky blue—
Is past the valley-sleepers, south or west.
—As I have trod the rumorous midnights, too,

And past the circuit of the lamp's thin flame
(O Nights that brought me to her body bare!)
Have dreamed beyond the print that bound her name.
Trains sounding the long blizzards out—I heard
Wail into distances I knew were hers.
Papooses crying on the wind's long mane
Screamed redskin dynasties that fled the brain,
—Dead echoes! But I knew her body there,
Time like a serpent down her shoulder, dark,
And space, an eaglet's wing, laid on her hair.

Under the Ozarks, domed by Iron Mountain,
The old gods of the rain lie wrapped in pools
Where eyeless fish curvet a sunken fountain   *nor the*
And re-descend with corn from querulous crows. *myths of her*
Such pilferings make up their timeless eatage,   *fathers . . .*
Propitiate them for their timber torn
By iron, iron—always the iron dealt cleavage!
They doze now, below axe and powder horn.

And Pullman breakfasters glide glistening steel
From tunnel into field—iron strides the dew—
Straddles the hill, a dance of wheel on wheel.
You have a half-hour's wait at Siskiyou,
Or stay the night and take the next train through.
Southward, near Cairo passing, you can see
The Ohio merging,—borne down Tennessee;
And if it's summer and the sun's in dusk
Maybe the breeze will lift the River's musk

—As though the waters breathed that you might know
Memphis Johnny, Steamboat Bill, Missouri Joe.
Oh, lean from the window, if the train slows down,
As though you touched hands with some ancient clown,
—A little while gaze absently below
And hum *Deep River* with them while they go.

Yes, turn again and sniff once more—look see,
O Sheriff, Brakeman and Authority—
Hitch up your pants and crunch another quid,
For you, too, feed the River timelessly.
And few evade full measure of their fate;
Always they smile out eerily what they seem.
I could believe he joked at heaven's gate—
Dan Midland—jolted from the cold brake-beam.

Down, down—born pioneers in time's despite,
Grimed tributaries to an ancient flow—
They win no frontier by their wayward plight,
But drift in stillness, as from Jordan's brow.

You will not hear it as the sea; even stone
Is not more hushed by gravity . . . But slow,
As loth to take more tribute—sliding prone
Like one whose eyes were buried long ago

The River, spreading, flows—and spends your dream.
What are you, lost within this tideless spell?
You are your father's father, and the stream—
A liquid theme that floating niggers swell.

Damp tonnage and alluvial march of days—
Nights turbid, vascular with silted shale
And roots surrendered down of moraine clays:
The Mississippi drinks the farthest dale.

O quarrying passion, undertowed sunlight!
The basalt surface drags a jungle grace
Ochreous and lynx-barred in lengthening might;
Patience! and you shall reach the biding place!

⟨ 184 ⟩

Over De Soto's bones the freighted floors
Throb past the City storied of three thrones.
Down two more turns the Mississippi pours
(Anon tall ironsides up from salt lagoons)

And flows within itself, heaps itself free.
All fades but one thin skyline 'round . . . Ahead
No embrace opens but the stinging sea;
The River lifts itself from its long bed,

Poised wholly on its dream, a mustard glow
Tortured with history, its one will—flow!
—The Passion spreads in wide tongues, choked and slow,
Meeting the Gulf, hosannas silently below.

HOWARD NEMEROV

LOW-LEVEL CROSS-COUNTRY

A railroad and a river and a road
Roughly in parallel though near and far
By turns and sometimes twisted in a thread

Three-ply with crossings-over, tunnelings-in,
And passing astern as soon as coming up,
With every slope and slippage of terrain—

And suddenly the town has been and gone,
The market square, the churches, and the schools,
The cemeteries and the swimming pools,

And out again, map folded on one knee
To read ahead, if there were time to read
With all the names aslant or upside down,

And over the rises and the deep ravines
Uncharted, lonely, still, and left behind
In the steady passage of the exercise

At the scope of speed and the escape of space
Down on the deck, perplexities resolved
Before they can be solved, and all the world

Flowing away the way it always does,
As if it were made of time, the thrice-wound theme
Of the railroad and the river and the road.

LOUISE BOGAN

TRAIN TUNE

Back   through   clouds
Back   through   clearing
Back   through   distance
Back   through   silence

Back   through   groves
Back   through   garlands
Back   by   rivers
Back   below   mountains

Back   through   lightning
Back   through   cities
Back   through   stars
Back   through   hours

Back   through   plains
Back   through   flowers
Back   through   birds
Back   through   rain

Back   through   smoke
Back   through   noon
Back   along   love
Back   through   midnight

MURIEL RUKEYSER

CAMPAIGN

"SUN ON THE FACES"

Sun on the faces. On the knotted rocks.
Sun on the iron. Sun on the dust of the roads.
The ravel of cloud, the silver chalkings of track
Lying westward through the dappled pass
South of the city where the mist flowed in.

Distance and the crowd.
The train goes dark-green westward

Over the free, light-gray crystals of rock.
Early morning the moment of thin air
4 a.m. and the cattle lying down
And all the cattle get up from their knees.
Early morning, the chill before the sun
And eleven men standing at a railroad crossing
The arm of the signal swinging Stop red Look red Listen.
Stop. People standing, looking separate in the morning air.
The little river over speckled stones
Passing the section crew. They wave. They wave.
The iceman and the gandy dancers,
And three blasts on the whistle for a penny.

In the smoke cities, sitting on the fences,
They shine in their leather, but they make no sign.
They hear the speaking in a pause of worlds
Roaring, in the haze roaring, in the stench
Of the slaughter of animals he roars. They make no sign.
In their stained aprons they listen, standing; they turn
Back to the cool immense bloodyards.
        His voice
Diminishing down the raspit avenues. Promises
Individual Man, but vaguely, and the vague cities
Promised, and downward through industrial
Illinois, vaguely, and
       through the blaze of town
Downstate, glowing, the summer leaves, the faces
Lit by September and inlit by the deep
Summer-end need for spiritual change.
        The hoarse raven
Croaks in his throat, Rock Island, the swaying
Train carries these panicky friends, advisors of symptoms,
Sending their telegrams.
*

The man sits in the rocking bedroom, claws
Hooked in his throat : anger and rage, pain
And refusal of pain. All right. Finally, Let him in.
But I don't need him.
*

From the throat he can rally strength. Remembering
Words to light home of track with the light of concentrated
Meaning and love past stupid pain.
But these are the towns listening : Galesburg, Joliet,
Peoria glowing, the ramshackle uniform and painted
Houses waiting : Missouri. He had puddled steel outside Chicago,
Where the huge fires roar, opening night, smoking
Pink smoke, yellow smoke, white, on the ochre
Air over Gary. Here, in broad dayland,
Had lain on the freights among the metal noises.
Hiss of sand, relief of steam, and a bell wagging
Where now the faces ring unanswerable
And the limitless ragged sunset
Serves only a man on the grass
Exhausted, in overalls, not hearing,
Or not caring if he hears.
*

There is a knotless line westward, past terraces
High on the roads, the black form of a car
Traveling under. Here, the clear glittering throat
The long pull of track that seals the black
Of quick sleep among the counting, among the hammering
Until the machine, blades whirling, dances the dance
Of Steel, and the machine chips and tightens and screams
A man saying, "A good steel rail will last."
A man saying, "He will need more than parades."
*

How was he first aware he would never walk again?
How did he ward off his mother's submissive hope?
How did he master his eyes? Unlock his knees?
Did he know the danger for his back and arms?
Did he suspect he might never have his hands?
And his hope? And his will? And his wife?
And the night visitations when the mutilated
Processions filled the world and his room of dream?
Water did this, the pool told him;
He panted, he swam : Water will get me out again!

Voice did this, Willkie heard the memory,
Voice, get me out again!
*

Street corner to corner he will talk all day,
Feasting on talk at midnight to the last
Listening man. In Willkie, the child's food
Made breath, the bread made word, where love
Is the word.
                    Doctor Barnard hearing
The rasping impossible voice under the beating light,
Rocking among the train : My God, I can't make him stop.
He goes right on night and day.
                                        Words traveling
Straight on the land. A train traveling, white
Plume over her back, over the rusty spurs
Never seen varnish; the network of glitter over
The network of track.
                        Down into Oklahoma,
Stretched beside overgrown dry creosote
Over the track, broomcorn, and again
The crowds at the tail platform,
Willkie talking : You mothers, you fathers . . .
*

The track cuts west. Slant roof, sun-catcher,
Outhouse, and barbed wire, the scrub growing up hill,
And a man in overalls walking the eleventh furrow.
The hard eyes of bigots. The hard eyes of the poor.
Full moon at Skelly Stadium, the crowd
Roaring through Tulsa, the screams of wild turkeys,
The underground black sounds of strength, Negroes and oil,
In a growing city. After the tents and clapboards,
The spinning of chance, the spinning dance of derricks
On the horizon through the pecan grove,
Across the broomcorn, across the tumbleweed,
Past the false-fronted clapboard, the pipeline, and this crowd,
Deep-throated, hard-riding, impoverished as by war,
Eaten away by dust the eroder, water,
Poverty the eroder and the eroder oil.
Waiting for fullness under the open moon.

⟨ 190 ⟩

I saw the footpath beside the telegraph poles
Waver among the knotted weeds,
Straighten. A child here
In faded clothes among the faded words:
The sheetflood washed me clean.
My hilltop when I ran alone
Is put to pasture, ridge the contour round,
How shall I be, how shall I be found?
Furrows hold ice, furrows hold snow,
Plow the slope that I name home.
Dust my mother overturned,
Sand and dust and wind have come,
To burn my days, until I go
To find the garden of the wind,
The pleasant garden of the world,
Where the sheetflood lost its force
Wrapped all its water in a bud,
Where bud and seed and fledgling bird,
Where the child will tell his word,
Where all the streams are from.
      *
I used to press tools in the Texas oil fields.
We produce 60% of the oil of the world.
   (Let the streetlamps burn all night!)

Amarillo in the morning heat
Away from the boom-town, infancy,
Used to be made of buffalo-hide,
Ain't made of buffalo-hide no more.
Little boys of the Panhandle
Used to pitch pennies at the yellow houses
Used to gather buffalo-bones.
Ship away the buffalo-bones.
Barbed wire was invented here:
Sing me a boardwalk in an old ghost town,
Gun play near the courthouse. Now vote me in,
I'll give a lot each for every vote,
Turn the LX into Amarillo,
Hot in the morning.

Down the Staked Plains the colored winds
Rising through mirage. The still
Elusive colors graze these hills,
Drink at these caves, go hunting in this sky.
The colors feed; or go hunting; or they hear.
Pause of colors before change.
A stranger, from the East, and talking fast,
Looks at a unique man,
The man from Tucumcari
Knows cattle and tourists. He stares at the candidate.
The great pure Apache watches from his eyes,
Ferocious dawns do climb the Walls of Bronze.
Two from Gallup remember the strike.
A carpenter from Conchas Dam,
A handful of people from Mimbres Valley,
Alamogordo, the Oscura Mountains,
A few curiosities down from Taos
Listen to Willkie.   Spit.   Shake hands.

Out of the throats of volcanoes : rocks : volcanoes
    forgotten : a word craggy and pinnacled:
Shiprock : the shape of a cry issuing : as people, as rock:
Among the rivers in a dry country : invasion of dunes, the
    white sand in the wash : from the cave waters
Given, erect crystals : pinnacles in the flows : a cap of lava
    over the rock:
Cliffs vermilion and undermined : retreating cliffs
For the rainwash, the sheetflood overthrow
Reaches them : they deploy, in summer thunderstorms
In the shale, in softness, until the softness goes;
The ruined villages of rock, and the people.
*
There they slept. They left the train.
Three planes from the plateau airport.
Through the low overcast into the phoenix sun.
Willkie then looking down, burned in his rage,
Hostile and sweating, saw the eaten country
Pinnacles into waves receding, the treeform famine
Of water vanished; the waves minimized to a ripple of terraces.

And all the people invisible.
Came down
To bleachers piled with local cotton and beef,
Hills of oranges, glass honey-hives.
*
The professionals see the signs in the dice, the signs in the
    cards and clouds,
Over their drinks they curse at the candidate, a renegade enemy
    whose sudden cause
Was rammed down their throats; he is wrecking their only chance.
The Dream of Business is a failing image.
Among the predictions, statistics, in the crowds,
The explosive seeds of defeat. Their deadliest fears
Run damp in their bones. More than torches by night,
More than pennons, candy, and speechmaking,
A campaign is slavery, they say,
The tiring slavery : to plan, to counsel, to control.
Above all : to carry out.
Willkie shows courage. Willkie will shout.
Forthright, alone, he speaks his mind.
But the party needed another kind—
A man who will accept support.
No benefit here of party or plan.
Joe Martin sacrificed himself, wanting a giant to fight a giant.
—He's not a giant!
He draws his crowds.
Dead whales on flatcars draw their crowds.
Nobody votes for a dead whale.
*
Parades. Rattle of palm trees. The silver planes.
Statues : Prometheus and General Otis.
Searchlights demanding.

This is the journey into the people, asking for consent, for
    sanction, for belief.
Concrete parades, stabbings and fortunetelling,
Gin, roughage, the studios on Christmas Eve, spotlit groceries
    and the prayer marathon.

The rose window copied from Rheims, the Aztec temple designed
    by the architect who believes in function.
Great ancient lizards and tar pits, the skeletons of pale fine starlets,
Some Rembrandts, a cafeteria (white tile and potassium broth)
Where you pay what you think the meal was worth.
The Strip, the Bowl, the Derby, the Easter Cross,
The Troc, the Wee Kirk; the neon in the graveyard,
Saying on and off, Father. On and off. On and off.
The oil well in the sea.
    *

They pray. Security against oldness
And death—for the gilding of all things.
Under the lights. On the porches, rocking, and at the Iowa
    picnic.
Drugged by wanhope, seduction, or the drugs.
Among the filling stations, between the orange trees,
Burst with illusion, listening for the faint
Tympans of rumor. Fame. Disaster. Or the sudden
Wild nimbus that cheats prediction and the grave.
A tower of linked intestines, cemented, climbing
Over the orange faces, digesting the world.
It cannot; it turns to digest itself.

But the incredible fifteen-year-old
Uncorrupt in her moment, standing at Vine.
    *

¶*From the Committee to Aid Migratory Workers:*
        We were accused of contributing to radical causes.
        When you are told a person is sick or in need,
        You don't ask him his religion, nationality or politics . . .
    *

        They will be obsessed by the word "security."
    *

¶*When Hollywood gets aroused, it gets aroused.*
¶*This is not a campaign. It's a crusade.*
—*Willkie at Long Beach*
    *

Up past the burnt hills. Distance and the crowd,
The track, development, the tracks on their light-gray crystal,

The knotless, nodeless line. Struck into water-light.
No but knotted, cloved, notched, scarred, traveled brightened
    by tears,
Good steel rails and riding them
Development riding on the tracks of law.
North in a ravel of cloud, into
The dappled pass south of the city.
Mist flowing over toward San Francisco
The power towers walking, Spaniards' ghosts,
The silver-white unborn.
            *
A network that emerges. At the ocean
Two musics tighten, floating gongs, bells inward
From the network to the eyes of a man
Whose pulse burns in his blue eyes when he sees the bridge.
            *
A red bridge fastening this city to the forest,
Telling relationship in a stroke of steel;
Cloud-hung among the mist it speaks the real,
In the morning of need asserts the purest
Of our connections : for the opposites
To call direct, to be the word that goes,
Glowing from fires of thought to thought's dense snows,
Growing among the treason and the threats.

Between the summer strung and the young city,
Linking the stonefall to the treefall slope,
Beyond the old namings of body and mind
A red bridge building a new-made identity:
Communion of love opened to cross and find
Self the enemy, this moment and our hope.
            *
Power never dominion.
Some other power.
Some force flaking in light, avalanches of lilies,
Days and the sun renewed in semen, pure
Among the uncorrupted fires, fire's ancestor,
Forgotten; worshipped secretly;
Where the vestigial Lucifer regales

Craters of memory; where leans
Some fleshly girl, the shaped stones of desire
Leaping in color at her human cunt.
They will translate this girl. She will appear
In textbooks as a sacrificed antelope
Guilt running shiny over the short fur.
Ideas of shame did split that throat.
But none of that is true tonight.
The girl was leaning over the crater, I dreamt it,
The shriveled flowers twisted in her hair,
And jewels budded at her throat.
The girl of choice, remembering the past fires,
Praising the word, the columns in the grove,
Arbor vitae uterinae
Locked in such branches, light in the dense forest,
Praising the world unknown and feeling beat
Among her branches
A human child.
Brambles of sense! and that responding power
Rocking the fullness of time.
Until it shall be, what never was:
River and born and dream.
Canals of music downward serenade
New satin gleams under her haunches;
And, running laterally,
And backwards across ripples,
Passing the lower stairs,
Even above the unforgettable murmur,
The sound of oars.

Body of the splendid, bear me now!
Completed by orbits of unhorsèd comets,
The bronze, paternal stars.

Cave of their messengers,
Thalamic cleft where the divorcèd myth
Begged to be nursed through hysteria that leap year,
Sank at the window—O the famous view!

This side or that side of the balcony
Falling, the graceless sanatorium swan,
Breaking nobody's kneecaps but her own.

Passes the pear orchard near the middle hill
At the wind's moment when all sails are lowered,
A small bird kiares, slope of his flight, the blue
Yielding flutes of his feathers, that small wing
Bounds us above—kiar! Inscribing our horizon.
A high note over our necessity.
*
A filament carrying morning through the waves,
A nerve singing branches.
Orbits of pear blossom
Recurring while the wars declared themselves;
On the red rails, the train hurling his words
Down all the arteries of tears.

Endure, grandmother of all music,
Crystal in Asia, indelible pinnacles
Color of going to sleep
Above the breastës gold.
Endure, sing : deep night in Abyssinia
Waits for a messenger, heat
Of that ancient waiting
Rising from tongues of lions.
The jagged time, the jagged time of clues,
All broken inheritances riding home
Past columns and ruins, down the edge-lit clouds
Reaching back to the well at home, a twilight girl
Wherefrom new breasts, new sources, feed the dawn.
Singing develop
The sapphire climbing song
Flaring, a woman's eternal jugular cry.
An Ethiopian Jew praising the world,
The flying psalm inviting creation come.

Osiris in his veins praising the world away.

Wine that is poetry—inclare! inclare!
The conqueror of all attractive dragons
Is in that vice and white and steam.

He waited. He saw the water.
But the recurrent branch
Flew backward on the track in early day,
Warning him against compliance, breaking
In blossom said, Willkie!
You must defy them or be lost!
The foam spinning on water straight beneath
Will tell another myth, and spin and drown.
Far down under the trestle invisible.
His sense of the real leaves him. Dizzy and blind.
Will go to Washington.

THE YOUNG MEN

The surface shine, the inner steel of track
Carry September ringing to a boy
Miles down and decades past, a maroon sweater
Haunting a plexus of rails.
A spur leading nowhere.
And silos, like ill-launched rockets, hurling tall
Such faulty upright weight five miles downtrack
As feeds the colored cattle, as feeds the governor,
As feeds the party wheelhorse as feeds me.

Ascending ties, a hymn of ladders. Colder.
I urge my wretched urgings clamber out,
Holding the frozen ironwork.
Coldbitten indecent lavender and white,
The naked noses and naked stares recede.
I hear the patching words that ring like coin
Behind the platform, my penny monument.

At a certain moment the railway forfeits metal,
Speed seizes this track, we are going fast.

The calendar's contagions, days, declarations,
Flaunted away on a Hollywood montage.
There must be a darkened third-run movie house
Behind that ice-clad coalyard where they show
Quiet. A willow. Some hammock-pampered girl
In a Middle Western college; pipedreams of reassurance
And a low speaking voice.

Waterfalls
Narrow, behind me.

All the American rivers
Controlled into metal systems,
Narrow as rails.

Firing down endless, successful rapids,
The tiny inconspicuous steely rapids
This train, my dragon, a Cherokee canoe
Clipping back birchbark over carbon paper
Pouring the smoke of my statement,
Tobacco that is the barn-hung skins of prophets
Pouring smoke out, that hardens into scars.

Effigy and belief! The track flattening south,
Splits from before backward, far into silver,
Opening into the small lost villages.
Sidings of young men propped against sycamores,
With eighteen miles between any two of them.
Their hopes are hanging three feet above their eyes;
Their girls away at a dance; all their big powers
Lifted up, and alone.
Lost villages, my frontier; our crest and crown;
My brothers who will never vote for me.
My lost self who will never vote for me.
*
Until I stand on the January platform
(Bunting and boards), Connecticut Avenue
That lowcut archway into the histories.
Speaking the inaugurals of these same young men,

Declaring a specific amnesty.
Then, eighteen miles apart, the muscular young
Arrogant fools, the founders of our future
With their ideas of freedom as relation
To human process, will push their shoulderblades
Against their treetrunks
And rear, like a tidal wave upon Peru.

Some fool with space on his left hand and his right
Will stare down-track.
The free, watery, liquid rails
Will seal our fire across the seamless land,
Fusing, fusing. Fusing
A new age.
The streaming hours of man,
The plant spread to the green sun.

That's what it'll take; not anything like these
Seven long years of Washington afternoons,
Shaking official syllables out of my creases:
Pork-barrel and candy-stick.
*
Then I forget.
The star in the nets of heaven
Blazed past my breastbone.
Did I forget that fire?
I forgot.
In my net of growth, my words are unreal to me.

RICHARD WILBUR

IN THE SMOKING CAR

The eyelids meet. He'll catch a little nap.
The grizzled, crew-cut head drops to his chest.
It shakes above the briefcase on his lap.
Close voices breathe, 'Poor sweet, he did his best.'

'Poor sweet, poor sweet,' the bird-hushed glades repeat,
Through which in quiet pomp his litter goes,
Carried by native girls with naked feet.
A sighing stream concurs in his repose.

Could he but think, he might recall to mind
The righteous mutiny or sudden gale
That beached him here; the dear ones left behind . . .
So near the ending, he forgets the tale.

Were he to lift his eyelids now, he might
Behold his maiden porters, brown and bare.
But even here he has no appetite.
It is enough to know that they are there.

Enough that now a honeyed music swells,
The gentle, mossed declivities begin,
And the whole air is full of flower-smells.
Failure, the longed-for valley, takes him in.

EDNA ST. VINCENT MILLAY

FROM A TRAIN WINDOW

Precious in the light of the early sun the Housatonic
Between its not unscalable mountains flows.
Precious in the January morning the shabby fur of the cat-tails by
    the stream.
The farmer driving his horse to the feed-store for a sack of
    cracked corn
Is not in haste; there is no whip in the socket.

Pleasant enough, gay even, by no means sad
Is the rickety graveyard on the hill. Those are not cypress trees
Perpendicular among the lurching slabs, but cedars from the
    neighbourhood,
Native to this rocky land, self-sown. Precious
In the early light, reassuring
Is the grave-scarred hillside.
As if after all, the earth might know what it is about.

JOHN BERRYMAN

THE TRAVELLER

They pointed me out on the highway, and they said
'That man has a curious way of holding his head.'

They pointed me out on the beach; they said 'That man
Will never become as we are, try as he can.'

They pointed me out at the station, and the guard
Looked at me twice, thrice, thoughtfully & hard.

I took the same train that the others took,
To the same place. Were it not for that look
And those words, we were all of us the same.
I studied merely maps. I tried to name
The effects of motion on the travellers,
I watched the couple I could see, the curse
And blessings of that couple, their destination,
The deception practised on them at the station,
Their courage. When the train stopped and they knew
The end of their journey, I descended too.

MAY SARTON

AFTER A TRAIN JOURNEY

My eyes are full of rivers and trees tonight,
The clear waters sprung in the green,
The swan's neck flashing in sunlight,
The trees laced dark, the tiny unknown flowers,
Skies never still, shining and darkening the hours.
How can I tell you all that I have been?

My thoughts are rooted with the trees,
My thoughts flow with the stream.
They flow and are arrested as a frieze.
How can I answer now or tell my dream,
How tell you what is far and what is near?
Only that river, tree, and swan are here.

Even at the slow rising of the full moon,
That delicate disturber of the soul,
I am so drenched in rivers and in trees,
I cannot speak. I have nothing to tell,
Except that I must learn of this pure solitude
All that I am and might be, root and bone,
Flowing and still and beautiful and good,
Now I am almost earth and almost whole.

DONALD JUSTICE

TRAIN

(Heading north through Florida, late at night and long ago,
and ending with a line from Thomas Wolfe)

Midnight or after, and the little lights
Glitter like lost beads from a broken necklace
Beyond smudged windows, lost and irretrievable—
Some promise of romance these Southern nights
Never entirely keep—unless, sleepless,
We should pass down dim corridors again
To stand, braced in a swaying vestibule,
Alone with the darkness and the wind—out there
Nothing but pines and one new road perhaps,
Straight and white, aimed at the distant gulf—
And hear, from the smoking room, the sudden high-pitched
Whinny of laughter pass from throat to throat;
And the great wheels smash and pound beneath our feet.

CAROLYN FORCHÉ

ON RETURNING TO DETROIT

Over the plum snow, the train's blond smoke,
dawn coming into Detroit but like Bratislava

the icy undersides of the train, the passengers
alseep on one another and those who cannot

pace the aisles touching seats to steady themselves
and between the cars their hair is silvered

by the fine ice that covers everything; a man
slamming his hand into a morning paper

a woman who has so rubbed her bright grey eyes
during grief that all she has seen can be seen in them

the century, of which twenty years are left,
several wars, a fire of black potatoes

and maybe a moment when across a table
she was loved and as a much younger woman

wet her fingertip and played the bells of empty
glasses of wine, impossible not to imagine her

doing that, drawing the shade and then in its ochre
light, the first button of his shirt, the rest

the plants boarded up along the wide black river,
the spools of unraveling light that are the rails

the domed Greek church, the glass hopes of the city
beside one another; the man whose clothes

he carries in a pillowcase, the woman whose old love
walks into her eyes each morning and with a pole

lowers the awnings over the shop stalls of fruit.

JOHN ASHBERY
_____

MELODIC TRAINS
_____

A little girl with scarlet enameled fingernails
Asks me what time it is—evidently that's a toy wristwatch
She's wearing, for fun. And it is fun to wear other
Odd things, like this briar pipe and tweed coat

Like date-colored sierras with the lines of seams
Sketched in and plunging now and then into unfathomable
Valleys that can't be deduced by the shape of the person
Sitting inside it—me, and just as our way is flat across
Dales and gulches; as though our train were a pencil

Guided by a ruler held against a photomural of the Alps
We both come to see distance as something unofficial
And impersonal yet not without its curious justification
Like the time of a stopped watch—right twice a day.

Only the wait in stations is vague and
Dimensionless, like oneself. How do they decide how much
Time to spend in each? One begins to suspect there's no
Rule or that it's applied haphazardly.

Sadness of the faces of children on the platform,
Concern of the grownups for connections, for the chances
Of getting a taxi, since these have no timetable.
You get one if you can find one though in principle

You can always find one, but the segment of chance
In the circle of certainty is what gives these leaning
Tower of Pisa figures their aspect of dogged
Impatience, banking forward into the wind.

In short any stop before the final one creates
Clouds of anxiety, of sad, regretful impatience
With ourselves, our lives, the way we have been dealing
With other people up until now. Why couldn't
We have been more considerate? These figures leaving

The platform or waiting to board the train are my brothers
In a way that really wants to tell me why there is so little
Panic and disorder in the world, and so much unhappiness.
If I were to get down now to stretch, take a few steps

In the wearying and world-weary clouds of steam like great
White apples, might I just through proximity and aping
Of postures and attitudes communicate this concern of mine
To them? That their jagged attitudes correspond to mine,

That their beefing strikes answering silver bells within
My own chest, and that I know, as they do, how the last
Stop is the most anxious one of all, though it means
Getting home at last, to the pleasures and dissatisfactions of home?

It's as though a visible chorus called up the different
Stages of the journey, singing about them and being them:
Not the people in the station, not the child opposite me
With currant fingernails, but the windows, seen through,

Reflecting imperfectly, ruthlessly splitting open the bluish
Vague landscape like a zipper. Each voice has its own
Descending scale to put one in one's place at every stage;
One need never not know where one is

Unless one gives up listening, sleeping, approaching a small
Western town that is nothing but a windmill. Then
The great fury of the end can drop as the solo
Voices tell about it, wreathing it somehow with an aura

Of good fortune and colossal welcomes from the mayor and
Citizens' committees tossing their hats into the air.
To hear them singing you'd think it had already happened
And we had focused back on the furniture of the air.

THEODORE ROETHKE

NIGHT JOURNEY

Now as the train bears west,
Its rhythm rocks the earth,
And from my Pullman berth
I stare into the night
While others take their rest.
Bridges of iron lace,
A suddenness of trees,
A lap of mountain mist
All cross my line of sight,
Then a bleak wasted place,
And a lake below my knees.
Full on my neck I feel
The straining at a curve;
My muscles move with steel,
I wake in every nerve.
I watch a beacon swing

From dark to blazing bright;
We thunder through ravines
And gullies washed with light.
Beyond the mountain pass
Mist deepens on the pane;
We rush into a rain
That rattles double glass.
Wheels shake the roadbed stone,
The pistons jerk and shove,
I stay up half the night
To see the land I love.

WILLIAM STAFFORD

———————————

HOLDING THE SKY

———————————

We saw a town by the track in Colorado.
Cedar trees below had sifted the air,
snow water foamed the torn river there,
and a lost road went climbing the slope like a ladder.

We were traveling between a mountain and Thursday,
holding pages back on the calendar,
remembering every turn in the roadway:
we could hold that sky, we said, and remember.

On the western slope we crashed into Thursday.
"So long," you said when the train stopped there.
Snow was falling, touching in the air.
Those dark mountains have never wavered.

ROBERT FROST

ON THE HEART'S BEGINNING TO CLOUD THE MIND

Something I saw or thought I saw
In the desert at midnight in Utah,
Looking out of my lower berth
At moonlit sky and moonlit earth.
The sky had here and there a star;
The earth had a single light afar,
A flickering, human pathetic light,
That was maintained against the night,
It seemed to me, by the people there,
With a Godforsaken brute despair.
It would flutter and fall in half an hour
Like the last petal off a flower.
But my heart was beginning to cloud my mind.
I knew a tale of a better kind.
That far light flickers because of trees.
The people can burn it as long as they please;
And when their interests in it end,
They can leave it to someone else to tend.
Come back that way a summer hence,
I should find it no more no less intense.
I pass, but scarcely pass no doubt,
When one will say, "Let us put it out."
The other without demur agrees.
They can keep it burning as long as they please;
They can put it out whenever they please.
One looks out last from the darkened room
At the shiny desert with spots of gloom
That might be people and are but cedar,
Have no purpose, have no leader,
Have never made the first move to assemble,

And so are nothing to make her tremble.
She can think of places that are not thus
Without indulging a "Not for us!"
Life is not so sinister-grave.
Matter of fact has made them brave.
He is husband, she is wife.
She fears not him, they fear not life.
They know where another light has been,
And more than one, to theirs akin,
But earlier out for bed tonight,
So lost on me in my surface flight.

This I saw when waking late,
Going by at a railroad rate,
Looking through wreaths of engine smoke
Far into the lives of other folk.

CHRISTOPHER BUCKLEY

TRAIN IN THE DESERT——1916

Charcoal on paper
—Georgia O'Keeffe

And so it comes
shaving away the formless
dark with its dark form,
stripping the silence down
to a smoke of movement
pall mall down the iron
corridor of its two grey lines,
taking over this space

with the half-light
of some big idea
about ourselves,
as if we were sure
that this is progress
we've sent thundering
outward in circles of sound
for our own amazement,
as if we will matter
finally to the sand
and the sky's long view,
that haze traveling
continually about Time,
as if the hand of man
will outlast all this,
the world slipping darkly
off its wheels . . .

LAWRENCE FERLINGHETTI
─────────────────────

STARTING FROM SAN FRANCISCO
─────────────────────

Here I go again
crossing the country in coach trains
(back to my old
lone wandering)
All night Eastward . . . Upward
over the Great Divide and on
into Utah

over Great Salt Plain
and onward, rocking,
the white dawn burst
across mesas,
table-lands,
all flat, all laid away.
Great glary sun—
wood bridge over water. . . .
Later in still light, we still reel onward—
Onward?
Back and forth, across the Continent,
bang bang
by any wheel or horse,
any rail,
by car
by buggy
by stagecoach,
walking,
riding,
hooves pounding the Great Plains,
caravans into the night. Forever.
Into Wyoming.
All that day and night, rocking through it,
snow on steppes and plains of November,
roads lost in it—or never existent—
back in the beginning again, no People yet,
no ruts Westward yet
under the snow. . . .
Still more huge spaces we bowl through,
still untouched dark land—
Indomitable.
Horizons of mesas
like plains of Spain high up
in Don Quixote country—
sharp eroded towers of bluffs
like windmills tilted,
"los molinos" of earth, abandoned—
Great long rectangular stone islands
sticking up on far plains, like forts

or immense light cargo ships
high on plains of water,
becalmed and rudderless,
props thrashing wheat,
stranded forever,
no one on those bridges. . . .
Later again, much later,
one small halfass town,
followed by one telephone wire
and one straight single iron road
hung to the tracks as by magnets
attached to a single endless fence,
past solitary pumping stations,
each with a tank, a car, a small house, a dog,
no people anywhere—
All hiding?
White Man gone home?
Must be a cowboy someplace. . . .
Birds flap from fences, trestles,
caw and caw their nothingness.
Stone church sticks up
quote Out of Nowhere unquote
This must be Interzone
between Heaven and Brooklyn.
Do they have a Classified Section
as in phonebooks
in the back of the Bibles here?
Otherwise they'd never find Anything.
Try Instant Zen. . . .
Still later again,
sunset and strange clouds like udders
rayed with light from below—
some God's hand sticks through,
black trees stand out.
The world is a winter farm—
Cradle we rocked out of—
prairie schooners into Pullmans,
their bright saloons sheeted in oblivion—
Wagon-lits—bedwagons over the prairies,

bodies nested in them,
hurtled through night, inscrutable. . . .
Onward still . . . or Backward . . .
huge snow fields still, on and on,
still no one,
Indians all gone to Florida
or Cuba!
Train hoots at something
in the nowhere we still rock through,
Dingding crossroads flicker by,
Mining towns, once roaring,
now shrunk to the railhead,
streetlights stoned with loneliness
or lit with leftover sun
they drank too much of during the day. . . .
And at long last now
this world shrunk
to one lone brakeman's face
stuck out of darkness—
long white forehead
like bleached skull of cow—
huge black sad eyes—
high-peaked cloth cap, grey-striped—
swings his railroad lantern high, close up,
as our window whizzes by—
his figure splashed upon it,
slanted, muezzin-like,
very grave, very tall,
strange skeleton—
Who stole America?

Myself I saw in the window reflected.

VII. THE TWILIGHT

GRAY AS STEEL

MARK VAN DOREN

A DREAM OF TRAINS

As long ago they raced,
Last night they raced again;
I heard them inside me,
I felt the roll of the land.

I looked out of a window
And I was moving too;
The moon above Nebraska,
Lonely and cold,

Mourned for all of the autumns
I had forgotten this:
The low hills that tilted,
The barrenness, the vast.

I think I will remember now
Until the end of the world
How lordly were the straightaways,
How lyrical the curves.

TED KOOSER

CITY LIMITS

Here on the west edge, the town turned its back on the west,
gave up the promise, nodded good-bye to a highway
that narrowed away, and with a sunset-red bandanna
bid the shimmering tracks go on, go on.

Go west, young man, cheered Horace Greeley, and west
rattled the new country, rocking along through the sparks,
the cattle dying, the children sick, the limits
always ahead like a wall of black mountains.

But the steam cooled and condensed, the pistons rusted.
The dead weight of trunks thudded onto the platform,
bursting their leather straps. Generations spilled out
and we settled for limits: strung fence wire, drew plat maps

with streets squared to the polestar, passed finicky laws,
built churches true: the bubble centered in the spirit level.
We let the plumb bob swing till it stopped with its point
on the spot where we were, where we were to remain.

The frontier rolled on ahead; we never caught up
with whatever it was, that rolling wave or weather front,
those wings of cloud. The news came back, delivered by failure,
a peach-crate of rags, a face caved in over its smiles.

We thrived on the failure of others; rich gossip
flowered like vines on the trellises. On porches,
what once had been dream leaned back on its rockers.
We could have told them. We could have told them so.

The bean-strings ran back and forth through the vines
defining our limits. Children played by the rules:
cat's cradle, Red Rover. Morticians showed up
with wagons of markers. The dead lay in their places.

Our horses grew heavy and lame tied to pickets
and our wheel-rims rusted and sprang from their spokes.
Fire-pit became city, its flashing red pennants strung
over the car lot. We signed on the line at the bank.

What we'd done to the Indians happened to us.
Our hearts had never been in it, this stopping;
we wanted a nowhere but gave ourselves over to gardens.
Now our old campsite limits itself on the west

to the lazy abandon of sunset—a pint bottle
whistling the blues in a dry prairie wind. Next to
the tracks, turning first one way and then another,
a switch with red eyes wipes its mouth with a sleeve.

THOMAS REITER

RIGHTS OF WAY

Its rails and the Main Chance gone to scrap
or Amtrak, this right of way
of the land-boom Kansas & Western

keeps a narrow prairie, a sky for raptors.
You've pulled over onto a farm lane
and found your way here among relict

rattlesnake master, puccoon,
compass plant and the three-clawed
inflorescence of bluestem grass

where it's 1874 and a sodbuster
who has just climbed down from a coach car
unfolds a surveyor's map.

When he looks up from piling cairns
to mark good ground for his house, windless
heat makes the prairie waver and jump:

a creek arises from stone, divides,
then braids itself like Easter palm;
on the horizon wild horses able to

carry giants. His flyer from the railroad's
land agent in Ohio, what
does it say? That rain will follow the plow

and that ordinary words and deeds
will pass from his life. A year later,
sod stacked into walls, unrolled on rafters,

he writes by tallowlight in his journal
that a thunderhead churning tinsel and foil
among fair-weather cumulus

has rained down mandibles and wings
that leave no crops or clothing whole
and scallop the edges of this very page.

When locusts flow across the rails,
Kansas & Western drive wheels
mimic windmills and stall the transit

of fresh grasslanders. What sinfulness
could have loosed such hunger on new life?
He speaks to no one he can name or imagine.

He speaks to you gathering seeds
along a forgotten right of way
to give your garden a prairie look.

DAVE ETTER
_____

RIDING THE ROCK ISLAND THROUGH KANSAS
_____

Listen to the Rock Island train
streaking across the Kansas plain:

Kansas City
Lawrence

Topeka
Alma
Alta Vista
Dwight
White City
Herington
Ramona
Tampa
Durham
Canton
Galva
McPherson
Inman
Hutchinson
Arlington
Langdon
Turon
Preston
Pratt
Cullison
Wellsford
Haviland
Greensburg
Mullinville
Bucklin
Kingsdown
Bloom
Minneola
Fowler
Meade
Plains
Kismet
Liberal

Goodbye to the wheat towns of pride.
Goodbye to the Rock Island ride.

LINDA PASTAN

AT THE TRAIN MUSEUM

Topeka . . . Junction City . . .
Santa Fe. The places
the imagination takes us
are simply these.
All . . . Points . . . East
the conductor calls
in that old plainchant

and a girl with a suitcase
steals down the porch stairs.
Rivers . . . Bridges . . . Cornfields
with stalks as tasseled
as the plaited hair of children
all over Kansas, falling asleep
to the loon-like call

of trains. I board
one more time, sensing
the quicksilver tracks,
how they branch towards a future
where I've long since
been carried, swaying
and only half awake.

JAMES WRIGHT

A POEM WRITTEN UNDER AN

ARCHWAY IN A DISCONTINUED

RAILROAD STATION, FARGO, NORTH DAKOTA

Outside the great clanging cathedrals of rust and smoke,
The locomotives browse on sidings.
They pause, exhausted by the silence of prairies.
Sometimes they leap and cry out, skitterish.
They fear dark little boys in Ohio,
Who know how to giggle without breathing,
Who sneak out of graveyards in summer twilights
And lay crossties across rails.
The rattle of coupling pins still echoes
In the smoke stains,
The Cincinnati of the dead.
Around the bend now, beyond the grain elevators,
The late afternoon limited wails
Savage with the horror and loneliness of a child, lost
And dragged by a glad cop through a Chicago terminal.
The noose tightens, the wail stops, and I am leaving.
Across the street, an arthritic man
Takes coins at the parking lot.
He smiles with the sinister grief
Of old age.

⟨ 226 ⟩

BRENDAN GALVIN

FOR A DAUGHTER GONE AWAY

Today there've been moments
the earth falters and almost
goes off in those trails of smoke
that resolve to flocks so far
and small they elude my naming.
Walking the old Boston & Maine
roadbed, September, I understand
why it takes fourteen
cormorants to hold the bay's
rocks down. Have I told you
anything you ought to know?
In time you'll come to learn
that all clichés are true, that
a son's a son till he marries,
and a daughter's a daughter
all her life, but today
I want to begin Latin I with you
again, or the multiplication
tables. For that first phrase of
unwavering soprano that came
once from your room, I'd suffer
a year of heavy metal. Let all
who believe they're ready for
today call this sentimentality,
but I want the indelible
print of a small hand
on the knees of my chinos again,
now that my head's full of
these cinders and clinkers
that refused fire's refinements.

I wish I could split myself
to deepen and hold on as
these crossties have, and admit
goatsbeard and chicory,
bluecurls and blazing star,
these weeds of your never quite
coming back. I wish I could stop
whatever's driving those flocks
and drove the B&M freights into air.

RICHMOND LATTIMORE

NOTE ON THE L & N

Bracketed by a diesel switcher and five
box cars before, and aft a red caboose,
with pistons pumping as if they were alive,
with eyeholes fixed ahead, cabhandles loose,
two old pacifics went
frogmarched to fate along the iron arc
that hooked the landscape to the edge of dark.

Dull on the wheels and ironed calm by time
the history of bright miles dies to the trip
of driving rods pushed from outside. They climb
in humped and prodded dead companionship
where the last curve is bent
and shapes them home. No more, in pride of steam,
will they thread out against the azure dream

of six o'clock on silver, past the sleep
of yards, the sleep of white grain towers, to raise
blue cities hours in future. Life is deep
dimmed in them, and their black is dull with days.
In a bewilderment
of motion they find aliens work their wheeled
stride to the scrapyard, and the ironmonger's field.

THOMAS MCGRATH
———————————————

THE END OF THE LINE
———————————————

The Iron Horse is rusting,
In the statue-fenced plazas of the nameless towns,
Who once crossed the wild prairies, cursing,
(Voice of feathers and smoke)
In his carbon rages, on his whirling shoes.

The mourning dove inherits his ancient voice;
But who will awaken the heroic sleeper out of his history—
That iron road to Noplace where he lately arrived
In a gunfire of oratory near where the soldiers lie?

Alas! Joe Hill, the millionaires have thrown your torch backward into
    this future!
Where now the locomotive is burning among the patriots.
Fourth of July. Hot . . .
    Daddy, what's at the end of the line?
    Baby, I tell you, the big train don't go there no more.

W. S. MERWIN

THE WHEELS OF THE TRAINS

They are there just the same
unnoticed for years
on dark tracks at the foot of their mountain

behind them holes in the hill
endless death of the sky
foreheads long unlit
illegibly inscribed

the cars
have been called into the air
an air that has gone
but these wait unmoved in their rust
row of suns
for another life

ahead of them
the tracks lead out through tall milkweed
untouched

for all my travels

CHRISTOPHER BURSK

TEARING UP THE TRACKS

There is sand where the tracks were
as if someone had lifted a river by its whole length
like a snake draped over the arms
and had carried the long coils of water
out of town,
removed the cool muscularity of the rails.

Although the trains had stopped, two years before,
our part of the tracks
stayed slippery from wear,
the wear of our hands on them.
We brushed our small section silvery
with steel wool, emery cloth, crocus cloth.

The rail left our hands sleek
and hard
as it vanished—everything which kept going out of our sight,
a river, a railroad,
must be eternal. We polished Cohasset's little stretch
of eternity

and let it slide from our fingers.
Each afternoon, it was a new length slithering
out of the past,
and we shined it once more and sent it into the future.
We didn't have to follow it,
the woods did.

Wherever the serpent rose along its own rippling hills,
trees were on both sides.

Like a river, it was guarded by what grew around it.
These were the days we owed loyalty
to nothing but empty track
to a resolute uselessness sunning itself in the sand.

Though the trains no more chose our town
and the tracks ran on pointlessly,
and though our parents forbade us to meet here,
we lay in the warm sand
between sleepers and smoked blades of grass down to the root.
This was our railroad now.

To get rid of these tracks
would be like trying to remove the spine from a man
without killing him,
like lifting a river out of a town.
But it was done.
And we were not there, the day the crossties were torn up,

The rails were sold for scrap.
Old serpent,
old purposelessness,
now we know the other way things disappear
besides that sharp corner
your track kept turning to eternity.

WILLIAM HEYEN

THE TIE

"Note old chestnut tie in foreground,"
the caption says. This photograph, in black and white,
in a railroad bulletin,
holds the old bed, overgrown, looking west,
of the New York & Pennsylvania line
somewhere in winter in an ash wood.
Our view is an intrusion,
so quiet is the snow-dusted glade.

Above the tie and past it, and in this section spoken,
when not to you, to no one, what could have been
rails' vanishing point is hidden in limbs.
Only the one visible tie, in all this stillness, hums,
but when we stare for a long time,
we stand in center picture as the last train
pulls away, saplings appearing within our hearing
behind it. . . . The tie, of course,

in this photographic meditation—
note the way it sheds snow, note
pith-rot shadows rising from inside it—
remembers nothing, not the rain of its own leaves,
not one soldier, not even the last caboose passing
into the light of dead time above it.
But we do, even as we remember nothing,
as we stare, as we may or may not want to.

ED OCHESTER

THE PENN CENTRAL STATION AT BEACON, N.Y.

An immense room as quiet
as an elephant graveyard
without spines or tusks.
Dust in the slantlight from windows
twenty feet up the wall.
Yesterday's *Times* for sale.
The stationmaster in a green eyeshade
snoozing or dead.
Below the clock an American flag.
Twice a day empty trains
go by without stopping—
Eisenhower Eisenhower Eisenhower Eisenhower—
one-eyed trains twice a night—
FDR & FDR & FDR & FDR—
shuttle between
Albany Albany Albany Albany
Manhattan Manhattan Manhattan Manhattan

LOREN EISELEY

AND AS FOR MAN

For W. H. Auden

In the railroad yards, leaving the city of darkness,
   leaving behind the platforms and the cries
   of baggagemen, freight handlers, redcaps,
I glance straight upward at a wall that holds
   the city back from the passage beneath the river.
   Huge power lines are guarded here; they feed
the locomotive's heart and the importunate voices that run
ahead of the speeding train with warnings of war and death,
                    or even love, to any desperate one.
I catch, before we enter the tunnel, light on the grey wall
                    none can climb.
Far up is a small ledge, sowed by the wind with ragweed—
        ragweed, beggar's-tick, foxtail,
        all that clings where man
        has his dominion and nothing,
        nothing is ever intended to grow,
        and supposedly nothing can.
Man would scythe them down if he could;
   man would poison them if he could reach so high,
but they live, incredibly they live, between the tunnel's darkness
                 and the sky.
This is how I shall remember New York forever:
not by the towers touching the evening star,
not by the lights in windows, not by lonely and driven men
shall I recall that city, but by the weeds
   undaunted on sheer stone and waiting,
showering their seed and waiting,
   waiting for the last train to enter the tunnel, waiting
for the last voice to speak on the telephonic track.

They will start to climb then, they will have had enough of waiting,
    and as for man, he will not be coming back.

LINDA PASTAN
_____

THE LAST TRAIN
_____

> The long-distance passenger train has moved one step nearer
> to extinction: on July 26 the New York Central said it
> intends to discontinue all trains running over 200 miles.
> —U.S. News & World Report

There may have been a boy,
lying in a cabin in the subtle place
where field and plain each goes its separate way,
who fell asleep to the muffled drumming of buffalo
as, dark and shaggy as sleep itself,
they traveled past his window towards extinction.

Now in a house at the edge of the same plain,
another boy lets consciousness recede
on the receding whistle of a train
passing his open window for the last time,
leaving behind a spike or rusted nails
like arrowheads or pieces of dried bone.

So we are left,
each boy, each sleeper,
to the single, abstract tone of the jet plane.
We follow sleep as well as we are able
along disintegrating paths of vapor,
high above the dreamlike shapes of clouds.

⟨ 236 ⟩

C. G. HANZLICEK

THE LAST TRAINS

Soon the last trains will be backed
Into sooty yards and forgotten.
As one of them sounds in the night now,
It's sad to think of that ending.
Why not send them away with dignity?

Those that groaned up mountain passes
And somehow held the tracks on steep curves
Should be derailed into granite canyons.
Behind their waterfall plunges
Huge trees will drop like crossing gates.

Engines that pulled the endless lines
Of creaking gondolas heaped with coal
Should make a final run
Down abandoned mine shafts
To sleep at last in the dark of the earth.

Desert trains should be left on the dunes
Where the sand will sift
Through the torn shades on pullman windows.
The midnight calls of coyote packs
Will echo the whistles of their ancestors.

Those that were once mirrored on lakes
Should ride the smooth gravel beds
Where light is almost lost,
Hauling forever a cargo of carp
Through weeds that move with the water.

Midwestern trains,
The trains I waved to so often as a boy,
I hope to see driven like cattle
Into the long grass of the plains
To graze into rust.

ARCHIBALD MACLEISH

GRAZING LOCOMOTIVES

Huge upon the hazy plain
Where bloom the momentary trees,
Where blows immensely round their knees
The grass that fades to air again,

Slow and solemn in the night
Beneath the slender pole by pole
That lifts above their reach each sole
Enormous melon of the light,

Still sweating from the deep ravines
Where rot within the buried wood
The bones of Time that are their food,
  Graze the great machines.

ACKNOWLEDGMENTS

The editor wishes to thank Diane Mahadeen for her generous assistance in the preparation of the manuscript.

"Evening Song" from *Mid-American Chants* by Sherwood Anderson. Copyright © 1918 by John Lane Co. Copyright renewed 1945 by Eleanor Copenhaver Anderson. Reprinted by permission of Harold Ober Associates, Inc.

"Melodic Trains" from *Houseboat Days* by John Ashbery. Copyright © 1977 by John Ashbery. Reprinted by permission of Viking Penguin, a division of Penguin Books USA, Inc.

"The Traveller" from *Homage to Mistress Bradstreet and Other Poems* by John Berryman. Copyright © 1968 by John Berryman. Reprinted by permission of Farrar, Straus and Giroux, Inc.

"The Beulah Railway" from *American Negro Folk-Songs* by Newman White. Copyright © 1928 by the President and Fellows of Harvard College. Reprinted by permission of Harvard University Press.

"The Big Rock Candy Mountains" from *The Folk Songs of North America* by Alan Lomax. Copyright © 1975 by Alan Lomax. Reprinted by permission of Doubleday, a division of Bantam Doubleday Dell Publishing Group, Inc.

"Looking at New-Fallen Snow from a Train" from *The Light around the Body* by Robert Bly. Copyright © 1959, 1960, 1961, 1962, 1963, 1964, 1965, 1966, 1967 by Robert Bly. Reprinted by permission of HarperCollins Publishers, Inc.

"Train Tune" from *The Blue Estuaries* by Louise Bogan. Copyright © 1968 by Louise Bogan. Reprinted by permission of Farrar, Straus and Giroux, Inc.

"Crossing" from *Letter from a Distant Land* by Philip Booth. Copyright © 1953 by Philip Booth. Reprinted by permission of Viking Penguin, a division of Penguin Books USA, Inc.

"Stations" from *Available Light* by Philip Booth. Copyright © 1964, 1968, 1969, 1972, 1973, 1974, 1975, 1976 by Philip Booth. Reprinted by permission of Viking Penguin, a division of Penguin Books USA, Inc.

"The Southern Blues" by Big Bill Broonzy from *Long Steel Rails* by Norm Cohen. Copyright © 1981 by Norm Cohen. Reprinted by permission of the University of Illinois Press.

"Call Boy," "Long Track Blues," "Sister Lou," and "Southern Road" from *The Collected Poems of Sterling A. Brown*, ed. Michael S. Harper. Copyright

"Trainwrecked Soldiers" from *Selected Poems* by John Frederick Nims. Copyright © 1982 by John Frederick Nims. Reprinted by permission of the University of Chicago Press.

"The Penn Central Station at Beacon, N.Y." from *Dancing on the Edge of Knives* by Ed Ochester. Copyright © 1973 by Ed Ochester. Reprinted by permission of the University of Missouri Press.

"Coal Train" from *Anthracite Country* by Jay Parini. Copyright © 1976, 1978, 1979, 1980, 1981, 1982 by Jay Parini. Reprinted by permission of Random House, Inc.

"At the Train Museum" from *A Fraction of Darkness* by Linda Pastan. Copyright © 1985 by Linda Pastan. Reprinted by permission of Linda Pastan and W. W. Norton and Company, Inc.

"The Last Train" from *A Perfect Circle of Sun* by Linda Pastan. Copyright © 1971 by Linda Pastan. Reprinted by permission of Linda Pastan.

"Self-Portrait Approaching Promontory, Utah" from *American Light* by Michael Pettit. Copyright © 1984 by Michael Pettit. Reprinted by permission of Michael Pettit and the University of Georgia Press.

"Getting There" from *Ariel* by Sylvia Plath. Copyright © 1963 (renewed) by Ted Hughes. Reprinted by permission of HarperCollins Publishers, Inc.

"For Esther" from *Out-of-the-Body-Travel* by Stanley Plumly. Copyright © 1974, 1975, 1976 by Stanley Plumly. Reprinted by permission of Ecco Press.

"Poor Paddy Works on the Railway" and "Railroad Bill" from *The American Songbag* by Carl Sandburg. Copyright © 1927 by Harcourt Brace and Co., renewed 1955 by Carl Sandburg. Reprinted by permission of Harcourt Brace and Co.

"The Railroad Blues" from *Black Songs: The Forge and the Flame* by John L. Lovell, Jr. Copyright © 1972 by John L. Lovell, Jr. Reprinted by permission of Simon and Schuster, Inc.

"Railroad Section Leader's Song" from *Negro Workaday Songs* by Howard B. Odum and Guy B. Johnson. Copyright © 1926 by the University of North Carolina Press. Reprinted by permission of the University of North Carolina Press.

"The Southern Road" from *Poem Counterpoem* by Dudley Randall. Copyright © 1966 by Dudley Randall. Reprinted by permission of Broadside Press.

"Hear Ye, Dakotas!" by Chief Red Cloud from *Touch the Earth* by T. C. McLuhan. Copyright © 1971 by T. C. McLuhan. Reprinted by permission of Touchstone Books, a division of Simon and Schuster, Inc.

"Railroad Bill, a Conjure Man" from *Chattanooga* by Ishmael Reed. Copyright © 1973 by Ishmael Reed. Reprinted by permission of Whitman Breed Abbott and Morgan.

INDEX

⟨ 250 ⟩